THE
SCREECH OWLS
SCRAPBOOK

THE SCREECH OWLS SERIES

1. Mystery at Lake Placid
2. The Night They Stole the Stanley Cup
3. The Screech Owls' Northern Adventure
4. Murder at Hockey Camp
5. Kidnapped in Sweden
6. Terror in Florida
7. The Quebec City Crisis
8. The Screech Owls' Home Loss
9. Nightmare in Nagano
10. Danger in Dinosaur Valley
11. The Ghost of the Stanley Cup
12. The West Coast Murders
13. Sudden Death in New York City
14. Horror on River Road
15. Death Down Under
16. Power Play in Washington

THE SCREECH OWLS SCRAPBOOK

ROY MACGREGOR
Illustrated by Greg Banning

Text copyright © 2001 by Roy MacGregor
Illustrations copyright © 2001 by Greg Banning

All rights reserved. The use of any part of this publication reproduced, transmitted in any form or by any means, electronic, mechanical, photocopying, recording, or otherwise, or stored in a retrieval system, without the prior written consent of the publisher – or, in case of photocopying or other reprographic copying, a licence from the Canadian Copyright Licensing Agency – is an infringement of the copyright law.

National Library of Canada Cataloguing in Publication Data

MacGregor, Roy, 1948-
    The Screech Owls scrapbook

ISBN 0-7710-5602-8

    I. Banning, Gregory C. II. Title.

PS8575.G84S373 2001   jC813'.54   C2001-901260-8
PZ7.M33Sc 2001

We acknowledge the financial support of the Government of Canada through the Book Publishing Industry Development Program for our publishing activities.

Design by Terri Nimmo
Cover illustration by Greg Banning

Typeset in Sabon by M&S, Toronto

Printed and bound in Canada

McClelland & Stewart Ltd.
The Canadian Publishers
481 University Ave.
Toronto, Ontario
M5G 2E9
www.mcclelland.com

1 2 3 4 5   05 04 03 02 01

CONTENTS

Introduction	6
Wayne Nishikawa	10
Nish's Top Ten Reasons Why He Should Be Captain	22
Nish's Top Ten Stupidest Purchases	23
Travis Lindsay	24
Sarah Cuthbertson	30
Sensational Plays	35
Andy Higgins	43
Lars Johanssen	44
Wilson Kelly	46
Nish's Top Ten Dumbest Lines	47
Samantha Bennett	57
Larry Ulmar	61
Simon Milliken	64
Muck's Life Lessons & Coaching Tips	65
Jesse Highboy	73
Liz Moscovitz	75
Dmitri Yakushev	76
A Few Great Laughs	78
Derek Dillinger	89
Fahd Noorizadeh	90
Gordie Griffith	92
A Gallery of Unforgettable Villains	93
Willie Granger	96
Jenny Staples	97
Jeremy Weathers	99
Best Tricks Played on Nish	100
Mr. Dillinger	109
Muck Munro	112
Nish's Greatest Madcap Schemes	117
Roster Changes	126
Record of All Games Played	126

Some people might find "Tamarack" a funny name for a small town, but we think it fits very well. The tamarack is a tree that many people don't even notice, or if they do they think it's nothing but a scraggly kind of pine that grows around swamps and bogs. There are others, however, who think that at certain times of the year, particularly in the fall, there is no tree quite so beautiful as the lonely tamarack. It is unique, found in every province and the northern territories, and it is the only conifer that sheds its needles in late fall. There is something wonderfully stubborn about the tough old tamarack, and there are

all kinds of life to be found around it, for those willing to take the time and know where to look. Much like the little town where the Screech Owls live.

The town of Tamarack lies in the heart of Canada, the country that gave the world the wonderful sport of ice hockey. The place is nothing but a sign along the main highway to the travellers who stick to the bypass and fail to take the leisurely journey in through town along Main Street. Those who do find their way into Tamarack discover one of the prettiest little towns in Canada, a community built along a twisting river that runs between two crystal-clear lakes. The river forms a small bay at the edge of

Tamarack where, every winter, the town workers clear off a large, rectangular patch of ice and put out a couple of homemade hockey nets for the use of any kids, and sometimes grownups, who want to join in a game of shinny.

The river cuts the town in half, and the houses all lie along two hills. One of them is known locally as "The Mountain," though it's really only a small rocky hill. Tourists drive up it to take photographs of the town. It is particularly popular in the fall, when the leaves turn and the surrounding hills and countryside wear a magical coat of red and brown and yellow and green. There are even a few tamaracks within sight, their soft brown needles making the trees look like feathers.

Tamarack celebrates all four seasons, but the one that makes the biggest impact is winter. It begins to snow in November and is often still snowing in April. And it stays. People who live here have a choice: they can stay inside and hold their breath until spring comes, or they can go out and enjoy the season. They generally get out and enjoy it, with cross-country skiing through the nearby hills, ice fishing on the two lakes and river, and skating everywhere, from the ploughed bay to the frozen creek that runs through farm fields on the town's outskirts.

Main Street is where the stores are, and the Bluebird Theatre. There are several churches, which can be seen from the lookout on The Mountain, and a new mosque that was built only this year. The oldest stone in the old graveyard dates from the birth of Canada, 1867, so it's been a while since people first came to settle and live along this river. It is a town that never seems to change, yet is always changing. Families move out, families move in. A century ago it was all Irish and Scottish and French and English and German and Polish descendants, who worked in the logging industry. Soon Italians came to work in the leather-tanning factory, which used chemicals from the hemlock and tamarack trees in the neighbourhood. Eventually the lumber industry declined and the tanning factory closed completely. But the people who came here to work in those jobs stayed on.

The single biggest business here now is tourism. There is a large marina on the river, and several resorts and children's camps and hundreds of cottages on the lakes. A magnificent provincial park is only a half-hour away, and a great deal of the local business has to do with supplying the campers and canoe trippers who head off into the huge park each summer.

There are three elementary schools in town. The biggest is Lord Stanley Public School, not far from the arena downtown. There is a curling rink and two ball diamonds and, more recently, three new soccer fields that are used all summer long. The ice is taken out of the arena each summer and the town lacrosse league starts up. At one point, Tamarack was better known for its championship lacrosse teams than for its hockey teams.

All that changed, however, when one-time local hockey hero Muck Munro started up the Screech Owls. Muck had been a great junior hockey star and would have had a wonderful career in the National Hockey League but for a leg injury that forced him to retire early from the game.

A few years ago the local minor hockey committee asked Muck if he'd like to start up a competitive peewee team. The committee wanted a coach who was *not* a father of one of the players. Muck agreed to give it a try, providing the committee would agree to a few points. First – and this was opposed by certain members of the committee – the team should be open to the best boy *and* girl hockey players the town could produce. His other demands were simple: there was to be as much practice as play; no interference either from parents or the committee; and he would get to pick his own support staff. He asked Don Dillinger to serve as team general manager, and Mr. Dillinger accepted.

All the Screech Owls live in Tamarack. Some, like Travis Lindsay, come from families that have been in town for three or more generations. Others, like Lars Johanssen, have only been in town a few months. There have been a few changes to the team since Muck put it together, but by and large he has managed to keep the same group since atom. Travis Lindsay now serves as captain, with Sarah Cuthbertson as one assistant, and the big mobile defenceman Wayne Nishikawa as the other.

The kids themselves chose the name "Screech Owls." It was suggested by Sarah, who pointed out that the little screech owl is native to the Tamarack area, and that it looks both very cute and very fierce at the same time. Mr. Dillinger said he knew an artist, Mr. Banning, who could do a wonderful logo of a screech owl carrying a hockey stick.

But the best thing was the word "Screech," Sarah argued. "No kid who ever hears that name will ever forget our team."

They held a vote and "Screech Owls" won handily. Second place went to the Tamarack Tornado. One suggestion, "The Tamarack Nish Worshippers," received only one vote.

So Screech Owls it was.

WAYNE NISHIKAWA #44

PLAYER PROFILE

Position
DEFENCE
Height
5'4"
Weight
148 lbs
Shoots
RIGHT
Born
TAMARACK, CANADA
Age
13

They call me Nish.

I don't mind. Truth is, I kind of like it. There's three other kids in the school called Wayne, but only one Nish. Only one Nish in the entire world, for that matter – which is just the way I like it.

Make that one Nish in the entire universe. You never know what's out there, after all. But even if there is another planet out there with a town like Tamarack and a hockey team called the Screech Owls – even if it has a team with a guy like Travis Lindsay, or a big pain in the butt like Sam Bennett, there's no way that the top player, the best defence-man, the "go-to guy" when nobody else on the team can score the overtime goal, is going to be called Nish or look one tiny bit like me, even if I had three eyes and hairy tentacles growing out of my armpits.

Let me tell you a bit about myself.

I live at 21 Lorne, a small street that runs between King and Cedar and has only about five houses on it. I live with my mom. It's a small house, a bungalow, but we have a finished basement and enough space in the laundry room for me to keep a hockey net down there for shooting. We also have a small garage but no car. My father passed away when I was about two years old, and I don't really know much about him except he was Japanese. He was born in something called a "war camp," where his parents had to live during World War Two, even though they were Canadian citizens and had their own house – and my mom says he had the greatest laugh anyone ever heard. Maybe that's where I get my sense of humour from. I hate people who boast, but I'm the funniest kid in Lord Stanley Public School. Mind you, there's not much competition.

Here are the things I like about school: recess, lunch, the final bell, summer holidays, Christmas

SCREECH OWLS
Wayne Nishikawa

SCOUTING REPORT

POS.	GAMES	GOALS	ASSISTS	POINTS	PIM
D	43	14	47	61	60

"Nishikawa can win a game – or lose it – all on his own. He has that much skill and lacks that much self-discipline. A smart, puck-carrying defenceman, when he comes to play – a nutcase when he just wants to play."

holidays, March Break, ice storms, professional development days, teachers' strikes, and when I'm sick.

I'd list the things I don't like about school, but that would take me more than a week to write out. Besides, it would just make me sick having to remember all the dumb assignments and boring books and stupid rules you have to deal with every single day of school. Then again, if I got sick, I wouldn't have to go tomorrow, would I? . . . Hmmmmmmm . . .

Yesterday I got in trouble for drawing in my Language Arts assignment book. Mrs. Gamboni – I call her "Mrs. Zamboni" for obvious reasons – got in a huff about me "destroying school property" and kicked me down to the vice-principal's office, where I had to sit and do math equations the rest of afternoon. What fun!

They wouldn't even listen to me. What was our assignment? Tell a story about yourself. Which was exactly what I'd done. But Mrs. Zamboni hadn't bothered to look at my work or done me the favour of asking me what the art was all about.

What I'd done was beautiful drawings of "Nish's Greatest Goals." The between-the-legs "Mario" goal I scored in Florida. The flip-over-the-net "Bure" goal I scored in New York City. The "Muck Munro" lacrosse goal that won us the provincial championship. The "Shootout" goal I scored on a slapper from the blueline to beat the Russians in Stockholm. What more could she ask for? Every one of them was a perfect story about Screech Owls' number 44, defence, Wayne Nishikawa, Superstar, Superhero, Superhumble.

I am a misunderstood person.

I don't say that to get anyone's sympathy. It's a fact. Sarah Cuthbertson thinks she knows me – but she's not even close. That loudmouth Sam Bennett thinks she knows me. Ha! What a joke! Travis Lindsay thinks he knows me, and he's my best friend, usually, so I guess in a way he does, but in a lot of other ways he doesn't.

I met Travis Lindsay in kindergarten – Miss Robinson's class. I was disgusted with what I saw my first day of school. I should have quit right there. All these little runts were standing around wetting themselves and crying for their mommies, and one of the little boys goes running off to washroom and comes running right back screaming because he's caught himself in his zipper and he wants Miss Robinson to help him get unstuck. She freaks out and calls the principal on the intercom, and the principal runs down – the kid's hyperventilating at this point – and takes one look at him and calls the janitor, who comes in, checks out the situation, goes back out to his workshop, and comes back in wearing big work gloves and carrying a pair of pliers. Of course this almost throws the kid into hysterics. It only took the janitor half a second to get him unstuck, but by this point Travis and I were laughing so hard we were holding our guts and rolling around on the floor. We've been best friends ever since.

Trav and I do everything together. He's the first call I make Saturday mornings – he's never up – and we play a little street hockey, a bit of Nintendo, and sometimes head down to the Bluebird for a movie if a good one's in town and old Mr. Dinsmore has forgotten he banned us for life once again. My mom adores Travis – she thinks he's cute and polite – and pretty much lets me do anything I want so long as I'm doing it with Travis. Once, with Travis's help, I talked her into letting us rent and watch all seven parts of *The Blood Children*. I said we *had* to see it because we were working on a school project to show how movies that show exploding eyeballs and slimy monsters popping out of people's guts should be "banned completely." I don't think I could have pulled it off without Travis being there, but she fell for it so hard she even hustled off to Blockbuster to rent the movies for us – even though Blockbuster wouldn't have let us touch them if we'd shown up on our own!

My mom's great, but she's a joiner. She thinks a kid should be signed up for everything in the world. I swear, if they had a course in "signing up," she'd put me in it. I took piano lessons until I, very wisely, spilled a Coke into Mr. Wigglesworth's electronic piano and shorted out the keys. I took violin until I "accidentally" tripped one day and squashed my violin into a million toothpicks. She signed me up for dance, of all things, only to have the teacher – bless her heart – take one look in my direction and start shouting "Too heavy! Too heavy!" like she was being asked to carry me home after class. My mom got mad and yanked me out of dance before the rest of the kids even got their snowsuits off and their tutus on. Now, if she would only do the same thing for school . . .

WAYNE NISHIKAWA #44

I think of myself as solid, not heavy. Find me a defenceman in the National Hockey League who's under two hundred pounds and I'll show you a minor leaguer. I take a lot of grief from the team about my so-called "big butt," but let me rub out a couple of players along the boards in a big game and just watch how fast those same skinny little teammates are lining up to slap old Nishikawa's big butt. I think of it as an extra defender out there for the Screechers, but they think of it as some kind of easy target for some of the most immature acts I've ever imagined – and believe me, I've imagined most of them! But really, freezing my boxers that time in Toronto? And flying them from the flagpole that time we camped up along the Ottawa River? How childish!

Maybe my eating habits aren't perfect, but so what? They make all these jokes about me and my Egg McMuffins, and me and my secret stash of candy bars – but who saved their butts up in James Bay because he was smart enough to fill his backpack with Smarties and Kit Kats and Mars bars and licorice? Besides, as I had to point out to those dweebs, you take

a handful of green licorice, a Caramilk chocolate bar, a Twinkie, and a pair of Reese's peanut butter cups, and you've got your completely balanced diet – right down to your greens!

Anyway, back to my mom, the joiner. She then started putting me in sports. Soccer first, which is where I met Sarah, and also Data and Derek Dillinger. Travis was also on our team, and Derek's wacko dad was our coach. He knew nothing about soccer, but of course he doesn't know anything about hockey, either. He's just a great, great guy – kind of like a grownup who refused to let go of his childhood. That's where we were introduced to the Mr. Dillinger's "Stupid Stops." It should be against the law for parents not to have "Stupid Stops," just like they won't let you go anywhere without a seat belt.

I wasn't a great soccer player. I looked goofy in those stupid shorts, and for a while they made me play goal wearing my mom's garden gloves. I didn't much care for T-ball, either. T-ball isn't really a game for kids at all: it's for loud, out-of-shape dads who get to use their own kids as equipment.

But then, one day when I was just about to turn seven, I discovered the only game for me.

Hockey.

I can't explain it. You've got Tiger Woods and golf, Jim Carrey and funny movies, and Wayne Nishikawa and hockey. I dominate. Totally. It's been like that from the first time I slipped on a jock strap, had my mom tie my skates, and went out and scored my very first goal – against Jeremy Weathers! – in a scrimmage. That was the second time I ran into Sarah Cuthbertson, and she also scored that first time out. My goal, of course, was much prettier. I wouldn't be the slightest bit surprised if it made the SportsChannel highlights that night – but of course, I was only six years old and wasn't allowed to stay up and watch.

Once I found hockey, I wasn't much interested in anything else, no matter how hard my mom tried to get me to sign up for other things. A bit of baseball, maybe, and lacrosse later on, but that's about it. I'm headed for the NHL as soon as I can get there. "You'll need an education to fall back on," my mom keeps telling me, but I just laugh. I'll get drafted in the first round and sign a contract. I'll have so much money to fall back on, I can buy a school if I need one! But first I'll buy a Porsche, a beach house in Hawaii, a one-man submarine, a private jet, a home entertainment centre with a 406-inch TV, my own backyard NHL-sized hockey rink, a pet kangaroo, and my own private movie theatre so I can watch all the

WAYNE NISHIKAWA #44

restricted movies I darn well want. Maybe I'll even buy a South Sea island for Sam Bennett and Sarah Cuthbertson so they can go away and never bug me again.

One day they'll make a movie of my life as a young hockey player. Kind of an inspirational film for young kids who want to grow up and be like me. There's tons of great material. I almost died, you know. It happened when I crashed head-on into the boards – I say some guy tripped me, Travis says I tripped on my own loose skate lace – and Mr. Dillinger was

over the boards almost as soon as I hit the ice. I couldn't feel a thing. I was trying to wiggle my toes and move around when suddenly he's almost on top of me, his knees on the sides of my helmet and very, very gently making sure I don't twist or move or hardly even breath. He wouldn't let anyone else come near me until the ambulance got there and they fitted me with this padded neck and head brace before they lifted me up. The ambulance came right out on the ice! They took X-rays at the hospital and the doctors said I had a hairline fracture of the third vertebra and might have been paralyzed for the rest of my life if Mr. Dillinger hadn't taken such quick action. That's just one of the reasons why I love the crazy old guy.

There are just so many stories about me in hockey. I won the Quebec Peewee for us – and Paul Kariya, who is one of the greatest ever to play the game, presented me with the MVP trophy. Travis almost ruined it all by accusing me of lying when I said Paul Kariya was my cousin, but Travis didn't know I was just joking. Anyway, he kind of is my cousin, isn't he? Trivia time: Name the two greatest Japanese-Canadians ever to play the game of hockey. . . . See what I mean!

But I get blamed for a lot of things that aren't my fault. I make a perfect end-to-end rush and Muck benches me for nothing. I accidentally hit Sarah or Sam in a practice – hey, it's hockey, it's a physical game! – and they toss me off the ice. I take a hit from that jerk at summer hockey camp, Buddy O'Reilly, and who gets kicked off the ice? Right again. Me! Muck tells us to slow up and not score, and I get the puck and rag it end-to-end and halfway back down the ice again, and Muck benches me. As I said to Trav at the time, "What more can I do for this team?"

I tie up the games. I win the championships. I check the big stars. I play my heart out for them – and what do they do for me? They kid me about the stink of my hockey bag when I'm the only one on the whole team that

can actually prove I work up a sweat out there. They play childish immature tricks on me, too. They trick me into going up high on things when they know perfectly well I don't like heights. They trick me into eating stuff like moose nostrils. They thought it was funny when I got thrown out of that river raft because I was the only one brave enough to be up front paddling, and they didn't even believe me when I said I darn near drowned in a whirlpool. They didn't believe me when I came back from the Badlands – the only one on the whole team with enough guts to go out mountain biking on his own – and told them there was a dinosaur out there! And who turned out to be telling the truth? Huh? Well, kind of, anyway . . .

I take it as a compliment that they want to knock me down a notch or two. It just proves they're jealous, and when you see all those MVP trophies on the fireplace mantle, and all those championship ribbons hanging in my bedroom, and all those newspaper write-ups that my mom keeps in that

WAYNE NISHIKAWA #44

fancy scrapbook, you understand why. I carry this team, and they all know it.

And that's how come they take a picture of me after a bird's pooped on my head and don't tell me about it. That's how come they send me off for interviews that were never arranged. That's why they cut the straps on my pants when I'm being asked to score the shootout winner in New York. That's why when I teach them how to talk Pig Latin they start acting like they invented it. And that's how come when I invented a new yell – "I'M GONNA HURL!" or "EEE-AWWW-KEEE!" or "KAAA-WAAAA-BUNG-GAAAA!" – they all try and take it over for themselves, especially that Sam Bennett.

Some of them are okay. Well, actually, all of them are, I guess. But I still wish a few more of them could be like Annika, my best buddy from Sweden. When she yelled "EEE-AWWW-KEEE!" it sounded like she had invented it, not stolen it. I wish she played on the Screechers. Her instead of Sam Bennett.

Maybe that's what I like best about hockey – the people you meet. I made good friends with the Wizard of Oz when we were in Australia – Wiz, in fact, may be the second best peewee hockey player I ever saw. You know who the best is, of course. But the one person I'll never forget as long as I live is my very great pal from Japan, Mr. Imoo.

20

Sometimes you hear older people like your mom or a teacher saying someone is "one of a kind," but Mr. Imoo is the true "one of a kind." He's a toothless hockey-playing monk who spends half his life saving people's souls in the temple and the other half knocking them senseless in the hockey rink. He's my ultimate hero. He's also the one who taught me the magical "force shield" that let me make that bare-handed save in Nagano that won the game for us. Crazy, isn't it? Even when they put me in goal I'm still the MVP.

There's a movie in my life, believe me – a great movie. The Old Nishapoobah pulling off the World's Biggest Skinny Dip at summer camp. The Old Nishabambi skedaddling across Vancouver's Wreck Beach buck naked, with a couple of killer thugs chasing his bare butt. The Old Nishabilly mooning the entire world – heck, the entire universe, even that imaginary Tamarack out in the Milky Way – in Times Square in New York City.

An inspirational movie for every kid that ever dreamed of being the greatest hockey player ever.

Unfortunately, none of them would be allowed to watch it.

If they wanted to base it on my life, they'd have to make it restricted.

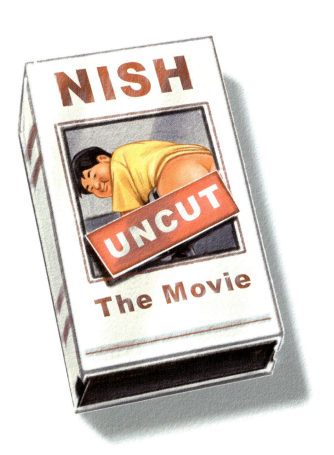

Nish's Top Ten Reasons Why He Should Be Captain

"The Top Ten Reasons Why Nish Should Be Captain," Nish announced. He was in his glory, a deep red colour moving up into his face and making him all but glow as he began his countdown. "Number ten," he began, "because he's won more most-valuable-player medals than anyone else on the Screech Owls."

Sam held up her hands to form a trumpet around her mouth and booed. Everyone laughed.

"Number nine," Nish continued, "because he's got the best shot."

"*Boo!*" several Owls called at once.

"Number eight, because he's Muck's favourite."

"*Boooo!*" more Owls joined in.

"Number seven, because he's the fan favourite."

"*Booooooo!*"

"Number six, because he's the only Screech Owl who'll ever make the NHL."

"*Boooooooo!*"

"Number five, because he's the best-looking of the Owls."

"*Boooooooo!*"

"Number four, because he's Paul Kariya's cousin!"

"*Boooooooooooo!*"

"Number three, because his equipment smells the best."

"*Boooooooooooo!*"

"Number two, because if he doesn't get it he's gonna hurl!"

"*Boooooooooooo!*"

"And number one," Nish announced, his eyes closed in private delight as he thought of his plan to moon the entire planet at midnight, "because he's the only peewee player in the world listed in the *Guinness Book of World Records*!"

"BOOOOOOOOOOOOOOOOOOOOO!!"

(from *Sudden Death in New York City*)

Nish's Top Ten Stupidest Purchases

1. X-ray glasses for seeing through bathing suits at the beach.
2. Plastic vomit.
3. Adult diapers so he can go to a banquet as a "Sumo Wrestler."
4. Pen with a lady in a bathing suit on it (when you turn the pen upside-down the bathing suit peels off).
5. A miniature tool kit to jimmy the cable around at the hotel so he could watch free adult movies.
6. Hair gel and mousse so he can look like Borje Salming.
7. Can of "Sweat" athletic drink.
8. Fireworks to blow up an outhouse.
9. Bucket hat, mirror sunglasses, and white sunscreen for "nudist" visit to Wreck Beach.
10. Knock-off Rolex watch.

TRAVIS LINDSAY #7

PLAYER PROFILE

Position
LEFT WING

Height
5'0"

Weight
103 lbs

Shoots
LEFT

Born
TAMARACK, CANADA

Age
12

Sometimes I try and imagine what it would be like if we moved away from Tamarack and I had to start at another school. I can see the teacher asking me to stand up and tell the class something about myself – but I can't begin to imagine what I'd say.

"Hi, my name is Travis Lindsay. I play peewee hockey. I was captain of my team back in Tamarack, and our team, that's the Screech Owls, went all around the world playing in tournaments. We had a lot of fun on the road. We've been involved in at least four murders, a kidnapping, a burglary, two attempted terrorists attacks, drug smuggling, and we've had to deal with dinosaurs, ghosts, and killer bears."

They'd laugh me right out of the room! Either that or carry me out in a cage.

Strange things happen to the Screech Owls – even when we don't leave town! I can't explain why. Maybe we're cursed. Or maybe it's just because we have Wayne Nishikawa on our team and things have a weird way of happening to Nish and anyone who happens to be around him.

For that matter, how would I explain Nish to other kids?

"My best friend back in Tamarack is Wayne Nishikawa. We called him Nish. He's part Japanese and part something else – I'm not sure what – and half the time it seems he hasn't got any clothes on. He calls himself the world's leading peewee nudist and he thinks he should be in the *Guinness Book of World Records* for having mooned two billion people at once at New Year's Eve in Times Square – only he never got to actually do it because we were too busy putting an end to a terrorist plot.

"Nish is a bit heavy. His big butt, he claims,

SCOUTING REPORT

POS.	GAMES	GOALS	ASSISTS	POINTS	PIM
F	43	36	35	72	4

"Smart, small left winger with a good eye for the right play. This hard-working captain is the team conscience."

is his best feature. He wears boxer shorts, sometimes – but usually he forgets to bring them with him when the team goes on the road. Sometimes when he does bring them he loses them – and once he found them frozen solid in the hotel fridge and another time he found them flying from the top of a flag pole. He has the stinkiest hockey bag in the world. Sitting next to him is kind of like getting sprayed by a skunk, but that's where I sit in the locker room – right beside him. He burps. He hangs noodles out of his nose. He makes farting noises under his armpits with his bare hand. He's sex crazy and thinks he can buy things like X-ray glasses and go to the beach and see through people's swimsuits. His favourite saying is 'I'M GONNA HURL!' – and he's the best friend I have in the whole wide world."

He is. I can't explain it. It seems like I've known him all my life, even though I know it's only been a little more than half. We started kindergarten together. I'll never forget that day. I've seen Nish turn pretty wild shades of red in my time, but never anything to equal that first day. He had to go to the bathroom, but was afraid to ask, and then the teacher, Miss Robinson, saves him by saying all the kids that need to go better go before recess. Nish heads off, but soon he's running back screaming his head off because he's caught himself in his zipper. He was screaming like he'd been shot, and they eventually had to get the janitor to come in with a pair of pliers – he wore his work gloves, too! – and get the poor guy unstuck. Nish now tells the story like it happened to someone else, but it didn't. It happened to Wayne Nishikawa, and I was there to witness it.

It wasn't long before we started walking to school together – he just lives over on Lorne Street – and we've been walking together ever since, except when we're having a fight over something, which is fairly often. Sarah lives pretty close, too, so all three of us became pretty good friends even before we ended up on the Owls together. Now I'd say out of my

best sixteen friends in the world, all sixteen play for the Screech Owls. I'd add in Muck and Mr. Dillinger, but it seems kind of silly for a kid to be saying he's best friends with grown men – but that's the way it is on our team. It's a very special team, and I love it.

My dad kids me about hockey. He says I'm a "traditionalist," which is a pretty weird thing to be when you're only twelve years old. But I think I know what he means. I love nothing better than natural ice, outdoors and hard. I love shinny, especially when Muck plays with us. Three of the greatest games I ever played – shinny

with Muck out in the fields, shinny on James Bay with Jesse's and Rachel's grandfather using the shovel for a goalie's stick, and shinny in Central Park – didn't even count, but I remember every single move and goal in them. I love just skating, the way it's almost like you're signing your name in the ice when you go out onto a fresh surface that still has a little wet film from the Zamboni. I love talking and arguing about the game – should you tape a stick from toe to heel or heel to toe? – and I even love everything to do with getting ready for a game. I love the ride there and the way I feel in my stomach when the rink comes into sight. I love getting dressed, except when Nish is acting the idiot. I like to think of myself as some sort of machine that's being assembled – underwear, protector, garter, left shin pad, right shin pad, socks, attach socks to garter, pants on loose, skates on loose and rest until I hear the Zamboni out on the ice, then tighten skates, tie pants, tighten belt on pants, shoulder pads, elbow pads, neck guard, pull sweater over head, wait, then helmet, click on face mask, gloves, stick, and I'm ready to go. Always the same order, always the same timing. Travis Lindsay, mighty hockey scoring machine, waiting only for Muck to flick the switch.

I also like summer hockey, which isn't very traditional. I love the way everything feels backwards about summer hockey. In winter you come in to the warmth and get out of your bulky outdoor clothes. In summer you come in to the cool and put on bulky equipment. In winter you're glad to get into the rink out of the cold, but in summer you like the rink because it's so cool and refreshing. Even your sweat feels different – cool in winter and hot in summer. But why that is I have no idea.

I have to admit, I love other sports in summer. I like to get out on my mountain bike and I can never wait to get up to my grandparents' cottage and do a little snorkelling. I enjoy baseball and soccer, too, but if there's one sport on earth that makes me feel as good as hockey does, it has to be lacrosse. I'm just surprised more kids don't play it.

I have two superstitions in hockey – one that everyone on the team knows, and one that only I know. Everyone knows I have to fire the puck off the crossbar in the warm-up, otherwise I won't have a good game. And if I put one off the crossbar with my very first shot in warm-up, I'll score in the game. I can't explain why it is, it just is. The second superstition is that when I'm dressing for a game I pull my sweater on very slowly and then, just as the "C" is passing, I kiss the sweater for good luck. No one knows about this because I don't want them laughing at me.

At least my superstitions don't bother anyone but me. Nish says his equipment must never, ever be cleaned. He won't even air it out. He also says he plays his best games right after he's cleared the dressing room with a big gasser – but his bag already stinks so bad it's a wonder anyone ever knows he's even done one. Except he makes such a big thing of it. Of course, he makes a big thing of everything.

Travis Lindsay 7

Another secret I have is that I spend a lot of time practising my autograph. I sometimes sit for hours at the kitchen table trying out new loops and ways of writing "Travis Lindsay." I always try and make it clear so anyone can read it – like you can read "Wayne Gretzky" so easily on anything he signs – and I always add my number, 7, just like they do in the National Hockey League. My greatest wish, as if everyone didn't already know, is to play in the NHL one day.

I don't talk much about my dreams, but I keep having the same ones, or at least almost always the same. The details might change a bit, but they're always in the same place with the same people. I dream sometimes that I'm up at my grandparents' cottage and something has happened to the water. Somehow during the night the lake has gone dry, all the water has vanished but for the odd pool of water and a lot of slippery mud. It's as if somebody has pulled out a big rubber plug in the middle of the lake and the water has drained away. It's so neat! Instead of snorkelling around the surface trying to see things on the bottom, now I can walk along the

bottom, picking up hundreds of lost fishing lures and even finding out, finally, how many lake trout are in there and if there really is a thirty-pound lunker like my grandfather always says there is!

Another dream is about finding my dad's long-lost hockey card collection. He once had complete sets from the 1950s – including a signed one by "Terrible" Ted Lindsay, the great Detroit Red Wings star who is his cousin. He thinks his mom, my Grandma Lindsay, threw them all out when he went off to university. But I find them in this dream. They're in the garage or in the basement or up at the cottage and I find them and it's a huge event – even the Hockey Hall of Fame in Toronto calls wanting to put them on display. They're in perfect condition, some of them not even unwrapped from their packs. There's Gordie Howe and Ted Lindsay and Terry Sawchuk and Rocket Richard and Jean Béliveau and Red Kelly and rookie cards of Bobby Hull and Frank Mahovlich – and they're all mine!

I also have this dream I hate where I wake up and I'm back a grade because the school found out they made a mistake passing me. Now I have to do last year's work all over again, and all my friends – Nish, Sarah, Data, Fahd, Sam, Lars, all the team – are a full grade ahead and no one wants to hang around with me any more because I'm just a little kid.

It doesn't take a psychiatrist to figure that one out. I'm always worried that I'm not growing right. I was the smallest player until Simon Milliken moved to town, but I'm still smaller than almost everyone else on the ice, no matter who we play. Muck says there are "big players who play small and small players who play big," and he says I play big, but it's not the same.

I guess I just have to be patient. I know I worry too much about everything – my dad says that's what makes me a good captain – but I can't help it. Being captain means a lot to me. I wore the "A" when Sarah was captain, but Muck gave me the "C" when she went off for a while to play for the Aeros women's team. When she came back to the Owls, I offered to give it up, but both Sarah and Muck said I was captain now and she'd be one of the assistant captains. I'm very proud of that "C" and I try to live up to Muck's expectations. I know sometimes I do stupid stuff, but I *try* to do the right thing. It's my job as captain.

Nish is our other "A." The joke on the team is that Nish's "A" stands for something other than "Assistant" – but I better not say what.

SARAH CUTHBERTSON #9

PLAYER PROFILE

Position
CENTRE

Height
5'5"

Weight
116 lbs

Shoots
LEFT

Born
TAMARACK, CANADA

Age
13

I don't hate Nish.

I know, a lot of people at school – and I suspect even a few of the Owls – think I do, but I don't. Not really. I actually feel sorry for him. I think he's a sexist pig, an ignoramus, a future maximum-security prisoner, a loudmouth, a slob, a fool, a jerk, a failed nudist, and the inside of his hockey bag smells like dead squirrels, but I don't hate him. Truth is, if we're going into overtime in a championship game, he's the second person I want to make sure is out there – because Nish, under pressure, is about as good a peewee hockey player as I've ever seen.

I say "second person" because the first player I want out there in a tight situation is me, Sarah Cuthbertson. Not because I'm the best. Not because I can "guarantee a win" or am even as much a scoring threat as The Big Stink (that's Nish), but because I just love it when everyone's exhausted and the clock is ticking down and someone has to do it – or else. When I feel Muck tap my shoulder in the last minute of a game, I think it's about as good a feeling as I ever get. It means he needs me, he trusts me, and he has faith in the fact that, no matter what, I'll try my very, very best.

Let Nish have all the glory – I'll take the responsibility, any time.

I hardly know how to explain my feeling for hockey. I love my family – my father and my mother and my sister, Meg, and my little brother, Edward, who my dad calls "Teeder" for reasons he's never explained. I love my town, Tamarack, because I know where I am at all times, I feel safe there, and all my friends live there. I love my friends – Sam and Travis and Data and Jenny and Liz and quiet Dmitri and, I guess (though I'd never say so out loud), even The Big Stink himself, a bit – and I love

SCOUTING REPORT

POS.	GAMES	GOALS	ASSISTS	POINTS	PIM
F	38	46	49	95	4

"The Owls' future Olympian! Graceful skater, deft stickhandler, good shot. Cuthbertson has all the tools and is the team's first-line centre."

my life and the seasons and my grandparents, especially when we go up to the sugar bush, and most, but not all, of my teachers.

But hockey? "Love" isn't a big enough word. My dad says when I was a little, little girl I use to cry because I wasn't a boy. I know how silly that sounds, but I wanted to be a boy more than anything in the world. I hated my name, Sarah, and I refused to wear dresses or ribbons in my hair. My dad says I even once put on his shaving cream and tried to shave when I

was four years old! But I don't remember that, and I have a hard time believing it. I think he's just pulling my leg.

My dad put me in all kinds of sports after I convinced my mom I wasn't interested in things like ballet. I played baseball and soccer and swam and did gymnastics and, one winter when I was about six, I asked my parents if I could sign up for hockey. My mother thought it was a crazy idea, but my dad was all for it. He even came out and coached us. Mind you, "coaching" mostly meant getting steel stacking chairs out of the lobby so we'd have something to hang onto while we were learning to skate around, and him having to run to the bathroom every few minutes with a kid who'd forgotten to go before putting on his equipment. But my dad liked it – and I adored it.

Skating came easily to me. I was one of the first to push away the chair and head out on my own, and I've never looked back. I just love the feeling, the sense of almost floating out there, and the way, with a couple of quick push offs, I can move from gliding around to full speed ahead. I love crossovers. I love skating backwards. I love the way my skates dig in after Mr. Dillinger has given them one of his special sharps and how I can look back and see every stride I take if I get out early when the ice is still fresh. I love the wind in my face. I love the way I feel after a game when I just loosen the laces and leave my skates on. They're more comfortable to me than slippers. Right from the start, skating has been the strongest part of my game.

I suppose I met Nish that first year. But I don't remember his big mouth, and I certainly don't remember any kid stinking so badly no one wanted to go in the dressing room with him. But you have to figure his mother was bringing him then and tying up his skates, and she'd make sure his stuff was washed and hung out to dry. It was probably the last time anything in that bag got within a mile of soap and water!

Travis I do remember. We got on instantly. He was a good skater, too, and really good with the puck early on. He was always friendly, always with a smile on his face, and I never once got the feeling from him that girls shouldn't be playing hockey. I sometimes felt other players thought that – or, more specifically, other players' fathers. I remember Travis asking if he could be on my line the first time we tried playing an actual game – really a scrimmage – and I've loved him ever since.

I remember I was watching television with my brother one evening and the SportsChannel started broadcasting the Women's Hockey World Championships. He was all set to turn the channel when my mom and I stopped him. There was Team Canada in beautiful maple leaf sweaters that seemed half pink and half red. And there was Team U.S.A., and the announcer said there were also teams from Finland, Sweden, China, and Japan.

It was the single most important thing I ever saw on TV. I watched and was absolutely amazed at how they played. They skated well and they shot fine, but it was such a different game. They passed beautifully, and all the time, and they seemed to be supporting each other like I'd never seen before. No one ever seemed to be angry with the goaltender if she let one in. No one tried to be a glory hog.

Just think, if Nish had been born a girl, women's hockey would have been an entirely different game!

When I heard that women's hockey was going to be played in Nagano, Japan, at the Winter Games, I took some white tape and put the number "98" on each of my skates. I don't wear number 98 – I'm number 9 on the Owls – but I keep it there still to mark that first year, 1998, that women's hockey became an official Olympic sport. My dream is to represent Canada in the Olympics and win a medal. I hope gold, but I'll take silver or bronze happily. Just to represent my country in the Olympics would be a lifetime achievement. That's what I'm aiming for. Maybe after that I'll become a doctor. Or maybe a vet. Or maybe something I haven't even thought about yet.

I try and model my play on what I've seen watching the very best women players in the world. Given a choice between a lucky goal and a beautiful passing play that sets up a goal, I'll take the assist. I love to be the playmaker. I also love to check. If Muck tells me it's my responsibility to make sure the other team's centre doesn't score, doing that becomes much more important to me than scoring. And I love the way our line works. Travis and I get to work on the passing plays, and Dmitri is always there as our secret weapon. Spring Dimitri free with his speed and his deking skills and, guaranteed, that water bottle is flying off the back of the net!

My greatest moment in hockey? No contest – the Quebec International Peewee Tournament, where I tied the tournament record with seven goals in one game. I thought someone had stolen my sweater for the championship game and had to go out wearing number 28, the extra jersey that Mr. Dillinger keeps in the equipment bag. I thought it was sabotage again,

someone trying to mess up the Owls like happened in Lake Placid. But no, it was just Mr. Dillinger sneaking off my sweater to the organizers so they could sew seven velvet pucks onto it – just like they'd done for Guy Lafleur when he set the record of seven goals – and then they had Paul Kariya, my hero, present it to me before the game. I wore it, seven pucks and all, for the entire match. The greatest thrill ever, for me.

I know I've been lucky. I was going to say a while ago that I wished more than anything else in the world for a chance to play in the Olympics, but that's not quite true. More than anything else in the world, I wish that my dear friend Data could come back and play for us. He's still very much a part of the team – and I thank Muck and Mr. Dillinger for that – but how I'd love to see Data back out on the ice, always there, always dependable.

Even if it meant he'd once again have to clean up on the ice after the biggest glory hog in hockey history.

"Nish's First Pavel Bure Attempt"

"The show's on," said Sarah, sitting beside Travis.

"I know," said Travis.

And what a show it was. Nish skated up and cut diagonally across centre, stickhandling beautifully. He had his head up, and Travis wondered if it was to see if there were any cameras on him.

Nish worked his way across the Selects' blue-line and down into the corner. He then faked a pass to Sam, who was charging in from the far point. Sam angrily slammed her stick onto the ice when Nish hung on. He had other ideas. He kept stickhandling behind the net, watching.

"Here comes his 'Bure,'" Travis announced on the bench.

"*Such* a surprise!" said Sarah.

Nish tapped the puck so it stood on edge, then lifted it high so it floated, spinning, over the net and over the head of the little Long Island goaltender.

Nish dug in hard, churning round to the front. He flew out from the boards and passed the left post moving backwards, away from the net, the puck still in the air.

He swung mightily, the play perfect – except for one small detail. He missed the puck, and fell with the effort.

A huge laugh went up from the sparse crowd watching in this little rink down by the East River.

Nish got up and chased hard back down the ice as the Selects managed a three-on-one break and scored on a good screen shot that ripped into Jeremy's glove and then trickled into the Owls' net.

"He's benched," Sarah said, as she shifted over to make room for the players coming off.

"Guaranteed," agreed Travis.

Nish came off, his face beet red, and didn't even bother looking over at Muck. What was the point? He plopped down beside Travis, ripped his helmet off, picked up the water bottle, and sprayed his face, hair and, a bit, into his open mouth. He swallowed, spat, and turned to Travis.

"What's with Muck?" he asked.

"You have to ask? "Travis said.

"I'm benched," Nish said as if it were an announcement.

"You're surprised?"

"Hey," Nish grinned. "He told us not to score, didn't he? What more can I do for this team?"

(from *Sudden Death in New York City*)

"Joe Hall's Heel Pass"

"I like what I see in you, Travis," Joe Hall said.

"Thanks," said Travis.

Joe Hall dropped a puck he had been carrying in his pocket. It sounded like a rifle shot in the empty rink. He stickhandled back and forth a few times, the straight blade as comfortable on one side of the puck as the other.

"You had a chance to win that opener for us, you know," Joe Hall said.

"I guess," admitted Travis. He knew what the young man was getting at. The drop pass to Sarah that didn't work.

"I want you to stand on the blueline," said Joe Hall. "And just watch something – okay?"

"Okay," said Travis.

Travis hurried to the blueline, sliding easily in his sneakers. He wished he was in his skates. He'd feel taller, more himself.

Joe Hall began moving away from Travis towards the net, stick-handling easily. He moved almost as if daydreaming, the puck clicking regularly from one side to the other as he moved in and stared, as if a goalie were there, waiting.

Suddenly there was a louder click – *and the puck was shooting straight back at Travis!*

It was right on Travis's blade, but it had happened so fast it caught him completely off guard. Travis fumbled the pass, letting the puck jump outside the blueline.

"How'd you do that?" Travis asked.

"Fire it back," said Joe Hall. "And this time be ready for it."

Travis passed the puck back. Joe Hall again stickhandled back and forth, the steady click of puck on wood almost soothing. Then the louder click – *and the puck was shooting back at Travis!*

He was ready this time, and could have fired a shot instantly.

"I still don't know how you're doing that!" Travis called.

"Come and see," Joe Hall called back.

Travis skidded on his sneakers to where Joe Hall was waiting. Travis gave him the puck and he stickhandled a bit, then he brought the heel of his stick down hard and fast on the front edge of the puck, sending it like a bullet between his legs and against the corner boards.

Joe Hall looked up and flashed his amazing smile. "'Rat' Westwick came up with it," he said. "He called it the 'heel pass.' He and 'One-Eyed' Frank McGee used to bamboozle other teams with it. They never knew when it was coming. Watch."

Joe Hall retrieved the puck and stickhandled again, effortlessly, and then suddenly the heel came down hard on the puck instead of passing over it again, and the puck shot, true and accurately, right between Joe Hall's legs and into the corner.

"Let me try," said Travis.

He took the puck, stickhandled, and chopped down, but the puck stayed where it was.

"You have to hit the front edge," said Joe Hall.

Travis tried again. This time the puck flew, but into his own feet. It wasn't clean and straight like it was when Joe Hall did it.

"It's your stick," said Joe Hall. "Try mine."

Travis handed over his new stick – Easton, special curve, narrow shaft, ultralight – and took Joe Hall's from him.

It felt heavy. It felt wrong. He set the blade on the ice, and it looked to the left-handed Travis like a right-hand stick. As if the curve was going the wrong way. But it wasn't a right stick either; it was perfectly straight.

There was no name on it, only "J. Hall" pencilled near the top of the handle.

"Where'd you buy this thing?" Travis said.

"You can't buy them," said Joe Hall. He didn't offer where it had come from.

Travis worked the puck back and forth. He lost it several times, being used to the cup of a curve that was no longer there.

"Try the heel pass," Joe Hall said.

Travis did. The stick came down perfectly on the puck, and it shot straight and true between his legs. Joe Hall was waiting and timed a shot perfectly with Travis's stick. The puck stuck high in the far corner of the net.

"Wow!" said Travis. "That worked perfectly."

"You like to try the stick in a game?" Joe Hall asked.

Travis felt the stick again. It still didn't feel right to him.

"Maybe," he said, looking up to make sure he wasn't hurting Joe Hall's feelings. "But I'm so used to mine."

Joe Hall took his stick back and handed Travis his. "Suit yourself," he said. "But you'll never master the heel pass with that curved blade."

(from *The Ghost of the Stanley Cup*)

"Nish's Mario Glory Move"

"Nishikawa, one superstar rush and you're on the bench," said Muck. "Got it?"

"Got it," Nish answered in a choirboy voice.

The Ann Arbor Wings came out with a little more zip this time and scored a second goal before the Owls took charge. But once they were back in control, the Owls slowly, simply, began to wind the game down. Muck didn't like it when a team – the Owls or anyone else – ran up the score on an outmatched opposition.

Sarah, in particular, was great at what Muck called "ragging the puck." She could hold onto it for ever, circling back and back until it all but drove the other team crazy.

"I'm gonna try a between-the-leg-er," Nish said to Travis as they sat on the bench after another shift in which nothing happened.

All winter long Nish had been trying to score a goal like the one on the Mario Lemieux videotape. The Owls all thought it was the greatest goal they'd ever seen: Lemieux coming in on net with a checker on him and getting an amazing shot away by putting his stick back between his own legs and snapping the puck over the poor goalie.

"Don't even think of it!" Travis warned.

But the next chance he got, Nish picked up a puck behind his own net and came up ice, weaving and bobbing, until he suddenly turned on the speed and split the Wings' defence. He broke through and came in on goal, Sarah hurrying to catch up. She banged her stick on the ice twice, the signal that she wanted the puck.

Nish, however, had other ideas. Letting the puck slide, he turned, stabbed his stick back between his short, chunky legs, and with a neat flick of his wrists managed to trip himself – all alone on a breakaway! Wayne Nishikawa's reach was not the same as Mario Lemieux's.

With the puck sliding harmlessly past the net, Nish, tumbling on one shoulder, flew straight into the boards, where his skates almost stuck in they hit so hard.

The whistle blew and everyone raced to see if he'd been hurt.

Nish lay on the ice, flat on his back, moaning.

"You all right, son?" the referee asked.

Nish opened his eyes, blinked twice. "You calling a penalty shot?" he asked in his choirboy's voice.

This time it was the referee's turn to blink.

"What for?"

"I got dumped on a clear breakaway, didn't I?"

Nish struggled dramatically to his feet. With the small crowd of fans applauding to show they were happy he wasn't hurt, he skated, stiffly and slowly, straight to the bench, where he walked to the very end and sat down, removing his helmet and dropping his gloves.

He wouldn't be getting another shift this game.

(from *Terror in Florida*)

ANDY HIGGINS #16

PLAYER PROFILE

Position
CENTRE
RIGHT WING

Height
5'6"

Weight
144 lbs

Shoots
RIGHT

Born
WINNIPEG, CANADA

Age
13

I got off on the wrong foot with the Owls.

When we moved into Tamarack from Winnipeg, I was trying to act like the cool Big City Guy and was looking down my nose at these little country hicks. But really I didn't know if I'd be able to make the hockey team, and I didn't know how I'd fit in, and I guess I tried to impress them all so they'd look up to me.

I certainly got their attention. But then I took it way too far. I stole some stuff in Toronto. This old woman was running the little store at the hotel we were staying at, and she was so shortsighted I honestly think she wouldn't have seen me if she was staring right at me.

I took this stuff – stupid stuff like chocolate bars and cigarette lighters and souvenir pins – and it sure did impress my new teammates. Impressed them so much that three of them went out and did the same thing and all got caught and sent home.

I cost us the tournament. We could have easily beat the Towers if Data and Fahd and Wilson had been there to play for us.

But I did put back the stuff I'd stolen. And I left enough money on the cash register to pay for whatever I'd eaten or used. She never saw that, either – but at least I did the right thing.

And after that I took it slow. I didn't push anymore. I didn't try to be the loudmouth – they already had someone doing a perfectly good job of that!

Now I really feel like I belong. I've become great friends with Travis and Gordie and Wilson. Even Nish, who is probably the centre of attention I wanted to be. But I'm glad I'm just Andy, the second-line centre.

SCOUTING REPORT

POS.	GAMES	GOALS	ASSISTS	POINTS	PIM
F	24	12	12	24	24

"The Big Shot – when Higgins winds up, with space, other teams run for cover."

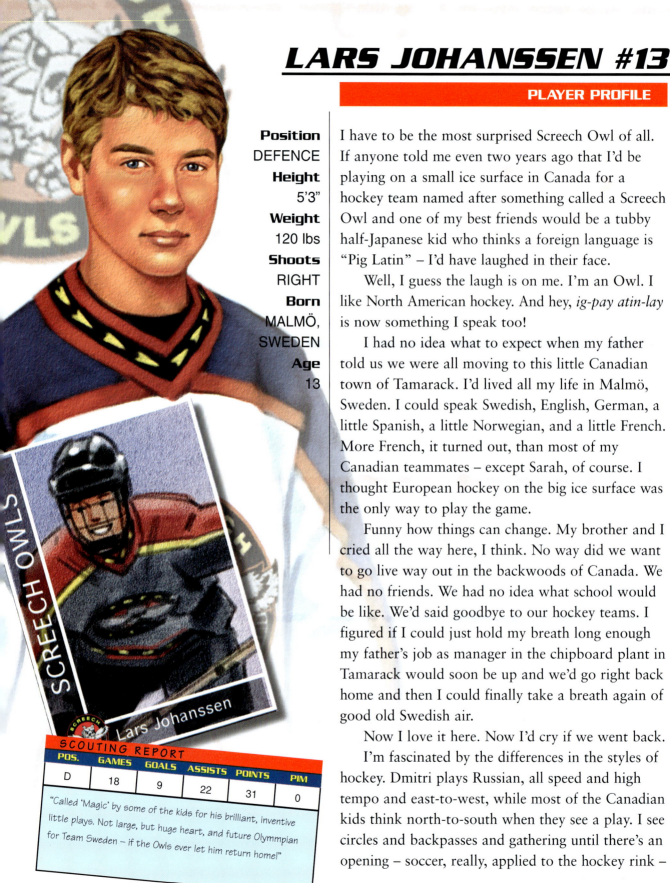

LARS JOHANSSEN #13

PLAYER PROFILE

Position DEFENCE
Height 5'3"
Weight 120 lbs
Shoots RIGHT
Born MALMÖ, SWEDEN
Age 13

I have to be the most surprised Screech Owl of all. If anyone told me even two years ago that I'd be playing on a small ice surface in Canada for a hockey team named after something called a Screech Owl and one of my best friends would be a tubby half-Japanese kid who thinks a foreign language is "Pig Latin" – I'd have laughed in their face.

Well, I guess the laugh is on me. I'm an Owl. I like North American hockey. And hey, *ig-pay atin-lay* is now something I speak too!

I had no idea what to expect when my father told us we were all moving to this little Canadian town of Tamarack. I'd lived all my life in Malmö, Sweden. I could speak Swedish, English, German, a little Spanish, a little Norwegian, and a little French. More French, it turned out, than most of my Canadian teammates – except Sarah, of course. I thought European hockey on the big ice surface was the only way to play the game.

Funny how things can change. My brother and I cried all the way here, I think. No way did we want to go live way out in the backwoods of Canada. We had no friends. We had no idea what school would be like. We'd said goodbye to our hockey teams. I figured if I could just hold my breath long enough my father's job as manager in the chipboard plant in Tamarack would soon be up and we'd go right back home and then I could finally take a breath again of good old Swedish air.

Now I love it here. Now I'd cry if we went back.

I'm fascinated by the differences in the styles of hockey. Dmitri plays Russian, all speed and high tempo and east-to-west, while most of the Canadian kids think north-to-south when they see a play. I see circles and backpasses and gathering until there's an opening – soccer, really, applied to the hockey rink –

SCOUTING REPORT

POS.	GAMES	GOALS	ASSISTS	POINTS	PIM
D	18	9	22	31	0

"Called 'Magic' by some of the kids for his brilliant, inventive little plays. Not large, but huge heart, and future Olymmpian for Team Sweden – if the Owls ever let him return home!"

and the beauty of Muck, our coach, is that he lets us bring all those elements to the game and tries to mesh them all together into one. I just wish we had a Czech kid on the team. Then we'd have every hockey style in the world!

It's been great fun. We went to Toronto, where my father was able to arrange for us to meet Mats Sundin at a practice. He's my great hero. I even wear his number, 13, on the Owls.

The Owls are a wonderful team, Mr. Dillinger is one of the greatest characters I ever met in hockey, and every trip somehow becomes an adventure. I thought it was absolutely insane when we went to Sweden and ended up getting kidnapped with Dmitri's cousin, Slava, but now I almost think if something outrageous didn't happen to us on a road trip it would be like we hadn't even played in the tournament!

Travis Lindsay is also a great person. He's got a wonderful heart both ways – as a good friend and as a good hockey player. I'd have him on my team any time. And Sarah Cuthbertson is, by far, the best skater we have. Some girls are starting to play the game in Sweden, but we don't have any Sarahs yet. My mother says this is strange, because Sweden has always led the world in equality of the sexes. But not in hockey. Canada's way out in front on that one.

But if Sweden still needs to get its own Sarahs, let's hope it never, ever, gets a Nish.

We may be the most open society in the world – but I'm not sure even Sweden is ready for nude grade six classes!

WILSON KELLY #27

PLAYER PROFILE

Position
DEFENCE

Height
5'5"

Weight
140 lb

Shoots
LEFT

Born
REGINA, CANADA

Age
13

Welcome to Team Jamaica!

That's what they call me! One player! I'm defence, forward, goaltender, coach, and manager – all at once!

I take a lot of kidding about this. It probably comes from that movie they made about the Jamaican bobsled team – *Cool Runnings*, I think it was called – and everyone says if Jamaica can find a bobsled team they can probably find a hockey team somewhere in the mountains back of Kingston. But let's not kid ourselves. It snows at the top of those mountains about once a century!

My parents are from Jamaica, but if I'm ever going to play hockey in the Olympics, it will be for Canada. And I'll do it with pride. I'll be one of those role players, a grinder, a guy you can always count on to be in position and ready to take every shift.

A real team player, in other words.

Unlike some others, whose names shall go unmentioned.

SCOUTING REPORT

POS.	GAMES	GOALS	ASSISTS	POINTS	PIM
D	43	2	3	5	42

"Big, stay-at-home defenceman, always dependable, always in position, always the first to cheer his teammates."

NISH'S TOP TEN DUMBEST LINES

1. The little blond defenceman was Jeremy Billings, the big dark centre Stu Yantha. Nish liked to know names, and liked to use them, too.

He went after Yantha halfway through the first period, with a face-off down in the Screech Owls' end and Travis on a line with Matt Brown and Gordie Griffith.

"Hey, Stu!" Nish called from in front of the net.

Yantha, waiting for the one linesman to bring a new puck for the other to drop, looked up, not knowing who had called his name.

Nish was grinning like he'd already scored. "I bet I know why your parents called you 'Stu'."

Yantha just stared, baffled. Nish hit him hard and low: "'Cause they couldn't spell '*Stuuuupid!*'"

(from *Mystery at Lake Placid*)

2. "Can we come in?" Travis called.

"In a minute!"

Lars yawned. "He's in a good mood this morning."

"I don't think he's feeling well."

They waited a moment longer. Travis tapped his knuckles lightly on the door.

"Okay, okay, okay!" Nish called from inside.

They could hear him fiddling with the lock. The door opened – and someone they had never seen before was standing in front of them! All they could see was the hair. Dark hair, standing almost straight up. Hair moulded into shiny, black spikes. Like stalagmites in a dark cavern. Still dripping with something oily.

"*Nish?*" Lars said.

Below the shining, black spikes, a big Nish grin spread across a vaguely familiar face.

"How do you like it? Just like Borje Salming, don't you think? A little mousse, a little Swedish gel – cost me less than thirty kronas."

Travis didn't know what to say. His hair was, well, bizarre. It was a bit like Borje Salming's, but this was also something entirely unique.

"*Well?*" Nish demanded.

Lars pushed by, giggling. He elbowed Nish out, closed the door, and locked it. He had to use the facilities.

"Well?" Nish said again.

Travis still didn't know what to say. He swallowed hard.

"I think you look like an idiot."

"You're just jealous," Nish said, pushing Travis out of the way so he could dress.

Nish's new hair was the highlight of the trip to Malmö. Sarah laughed so hard she had tears rolling down her cheeks. Wilson and Data stood behind his seat

48

holding their noses, for Nish's slicked head had a certain distinctive smell.

"We'll have to drill holes in the top of his helmet," said Muck, shaking his head.

(from Kidnapped in Sweden)

3. All eight Screech Owls scrambled up and over the high snowbank at the end of the lot. They lay on their stomachs, watched, and waited.

"I gotta be in by nine," Fahd warned.

"I'm good till nine-thirty," said Sarah.

"Nine."

"Nine-thirty."

"Nine."

"Nine."

"Nine."

"Midnight."

Travis turned to his side and looked crossly at Nish, who was beaming from ear to ear. Nish, the Man About Town, who would tell them he and his uncle sometimes enjoyed a good cigar after dinner. Who once maintained he'd driven the car around the block. Who in his imagination would stay up all night long, drinking and smoking and partying, but who would wake up in his Toronto Maple Leafs pyjamas in the morning and expect his mother to bring him in a bowlful of Froot Loops while he watched the Saturday-morning cartoons.

(from The Screech Owls' Home Loss)

4. "TOASTED BUNS!"

Travis Lindsay could only shake his head in wonder. The Screech Owls had been in Nagano, Japan, less than an hour, and already Nish was spinning out of control.

"WE GOT TOASTED BUNS!"

The Owls had just checked in to the Olympic Village, where they would be staying for the next two weeks. They'd been issued door keys, divided into groups, and assigned to different "apartments" in the large complex that would be home to all the teams competing in this special, once-in-a-lifetime "Junior Olympics." Travis was sharing with Dmitri Yakushev, Lars Johanssen, Andy Higgins, Fahd Noorizadeh – and, of course, his so-called, perhaps soon to be former, best friend Wayne Nishikawa.

"COME AND GET YOUR BUNS TOASTED!"

Rarely had Travis seen Nish this wound up. Travis and the other players had been carefully hanging up their clothes or putting them neatly in drawers, when Nish, as usual, had simply stepped into the bedroom he'd been sharing with Travis, unzipped his bag, turned it upside down, and let shirts and pants tumble into a heap beside his bed. Then he'd gone "exploring."

It took him less than a minute to find out that Japan was the land of the heated toilet seat.

"*Fan-tas-tic!*" Nish had shouted out in triumph. "*At least one country still believes in the electric chair!*"

The rooms were not very warm. The elevator and the stairs were all on the outside of the building, the wind-blown snow dancing around the walkways as the Owls had made their way to their little apartments. The apartments were heated, but still cool compared to homes in North America. Each bathroom had its own heater, and the toilet seat itself was wired for heat, with a small red dial on the side to control the temperature. Nish had instantly cranked theirs up as high as it would go.

"THIS IS BETTER THAN WEDGIES!"

(from *Nightmare in Nagano*)

5. Twice more the Ducks scored, and in the final minute they pulled their own goalie to try to tie the game.

Sarah's line was out to stop them, Travis hoping he might finally get a goal, even if it was into the empty net.

But the Sapporo Mighty Ducks had other ideas. They were flying now, and the good puck-carrier beat Travis and then Dmitri before putting a perfect breakaway pass on the stick of one of the Ducks' better skaters. He split the Owls' defence and came flying in on Nish, who went down too soon.

The Duck fired the puck high toward the open top corner.

Nish, flat on his back, kicked his legs straight up.

The puck clipped off the top of his skate toe and hammered against the glass.

A second later the horn blew. Game over.

Nish was last into the dressing room, his uniform soaked through with sweat, his big pads seemingly made of cement.

"I guess I saved your skins," he announced. "If it wasn't for me, we'd have been lucky to come out of that with a tie."

(from *Nightmare in Nagano*)

6. That night the Owls had a team dinner at the camp with the tournament organizers. It looked as if Nish was going to behave himself, until the visiting church minister suggested that, instead of a prayer before the meal, they go around the tables and tell the gathering one special thing in their lives for which they were particularly grateful.

"My grandparents," said Travis.

"My country," said Lars, who was fiercely proud of being from Sweden.

"My new friend and teammate, Data," said Sam.

"Mail-order catalogues," said Nish.

The minister, already moving his finger on to the next Owl, jumped back, his attention returning to Nish, a puzzled expression on his face.

"Why, son?"

Nish grinned. "I'm grateful for the lingerie ads."

(from *The Ghost of the Stanley Cup*)

7. Two of the Rebels' players, Kenzie MacNeil and James Grove, were the *Citizen*'s choice as most likely candidates for the Most Valuable Player award, which was to be presented on the final day by the Governor General.

If the award were to go to one of the two Rebels, said the *Citizen*, it would be "poetic justice."

"What the heck's *that* mean?" Nish demanded when Travis showed him the article.

"That it *should* happen. That it's the right thing."

"Yeah, right!" Nish said with great sarcasm.

Nish didn't miss a beat. Just before the puck dropped on the opening face-off, he skated past Kenzie MacNeil, lining up to face off against Sarah, and quickly whispered his own version of "poetic justice":

"*Roses are red, violets are blue.
I'll be MVP – not you.*"

MacNeil just looked at him and shook his head, baffled.

Halfway through the shift Travis could see why Kenzie MacNeil might be the early favourite as the tournament's top player. Joe Hall had switched the lineups around a bit, perhaps sensing that Nish and Sam would hardly be able to play together. Nish was out with Lars, and Lars made the mistake of trying to jump into the play right after the face-off. Sarah tied up MacNeil, but just as Lars tried to slip in and away with the puck, MacNeil used his skate to drag the puck through the circle and up onto his stick. Sarah stuck with him, but he was able, one-handed, to lick a backhand pass to his left winger, James Grove, who suddenly had open ice with Lars out of the picture.

Nish cut fast across the blueline to cover for Lars, but to do so he had to leave the far wing open. The Rebel left winger was able to fire a rink-wide pass, blind, knowing that the Rebels' other winger would be open.

Travis was the Owls' only hope. He chased his check and caught him just inside the Owls' blueline. Travis began leaning on the player to force him off towards the boards, but he should have tried to play the puck. The winger flipped an easy drop pass that looped over Travis's stick and fell, like a spinning plate, on the safe side of the line.

Kenzie MacNeil, moving up fast, was all alone. He came in on Jeremy – who was coming out to cut the angle – and instead of cutting, or faking a shot, MacNeil simply hauled back and slammed a vicious slapshot that tore right through Jeremy's pads and popped out the other side into the Screech Owls net.

As the starting lineup skated off, their heads hung low, Sarah said to Nish,

*"Roses are red, violets are blue,
When that guy scored, where were you?"*

(from *The Ghost of the Stanley Cup*)

8. The guide said any dolphins they saw today would likely be Pacific white-sided dolphins, which were common along this coast. Killer whales, she added, were also dolphins and could be found off the coast of British Columbia as well, though they were rarely seen. They might get lucky, but more likely they'd see a big grey, which was just as good, in her opinion.

"Greys are beautiful animals," she said. "Some of them are longer than a city bus, and once they get here they spend most of their time eating tiny little sea creatures they find in these waters. An adult grey will eat about twelve hundred kilograms of food a day – that's the equivalent of ten thousand Big Macs."

"*That's what I usually order!*" Nish shouted.

The dolphins, the guide said, prefer salmon, but also love a good feed of anchovies.

"They order *pizza* out here, with *anchovies*?" Nish screeched. "*I think I'm gonna hurl!*"

(from *The West Coast Murders*)

9. They drove down to New York in a light, wet snow that turned the pavement ahead black and glistening. Mr. Dillinger drove the old bus, sticking to the turnpikes and stopping only for bathroom breaks and lunch. He kept the music low, the heavy beat of the windshield wipers droning over everything, and soon most of the bus was asleep. Muck dozed in the seat closest to the door, a big book slipping off his lap several times as he fell into a deep slumber. Sam and Sarah slept with their heads tilted together. Fahd and Data played games on Data's new laptop computer until the battery ran down, and then they too slept. All up and down the old bus there were legs sticking out in the aisle, pillows jammed against windows, jackets over heads.

Travis got up at one point to stretch his legs. He looked towards the back of the bus, where much of the Screech Owls' equipment had been piled in the empty seats. There was a window on the safety door at the back, and he thought he might just stand there a while and watch the traffic.

Unfortunately, someone was already there.

Nish. His back to the window. Bent over almost double. His belt undone and pants down around his ankles.

"*What are you doing?*" Travis hissed.

Nish looked up, blinked a couple of times as if the answer were obvious.

"Practising."

"*Practising?*" Travis asked, incredulous.

"You practise hockey, don't you?" Nish said as he hiked up his pants. "Why wouldn't you practise mooning?"

Buckling up his belt, Nish stepped away from the wet, snow-streaked window. Travis half expected to see a line of police cars following them, lights flashing and sirens wailing. But there was only a van several hundred feet behind, its wipers beating furiously back and forth to fight the spray of the bus, the grey-haired driver staring straight ahead as if hypnotized by the road.

He hadn't seen a thing.

(from *Sudden Death in New York City*)

10. Passing for fourteen seemed to do something to Nish. He was even more outrageous than usual. Instead of sitting quietly in a corner of the movie theatre where they might go unnoticed, Nish insisted they sit dead centre. While they waited for the previews to begin, he made animal sounds, shouted out "KAW-WA-BUNGA!" and "EEE-AWWW-KEEE!" and once even passed wind loudly before holding his nose with one hand and raising the other high to point straight down at Travis.

Travis slid lower and lower in his seat.

The previews did nothing to settle Nish down. He whistled and stomped and clapped his hands. He began cracking jokes about the action on screen, and when some of the audience laughed, he got even louder.

Travis hoped desperately that Nish would settle down once the main feature began, but he was out of luck. *The Blood Children: Part VIII* started, and as Travis sank ever lower into his seat, Nish seemed to grow in his.

First head that got lopped off, Nish shouted out, *"That was a no-brainer!"*

First alien that popped out of a graveyard, Nish blew a bugle charge as if the cavalry were coming.

The aliens moved on some sort of jet boots that enabled them to float just above ground, and they carried vicious scythe-type weapons that twisted at the end like an illegally curved hockey stick.

It was too much for Nish to resist. When the aliens moved in for their first civilian massacre, he leaped to his feet, cupped his hands around his mouth, and yelled, "*Go Leafs Go!*"

Once he hit on this hockey theme, Nish was lost. In the movie's very first "romantic" scene – a long, passionate kiss between a gorgeous blonde actress and a handsome soldier who turned out to be a vampire – he shouted, "*Two minutes for no neck protector!*"

(from *Horror on River Road*)

SAMANTHA BENNETT #4

PLAYER PROFILE

Position
DEFENCE
Height
5'4"
Weight
130 lbs
Shoots
LEFT
Born
WINNIPEG, CANADA
Age
12

I didn't join the Screech Owls until they were headed for Ottawa and the Little Stanley Cup tournament, so I won't pretend to know everything about the team. But I do know that Nish can be an awful pain, and I kind of think I have two jobs with the Owls. The first one is to play defence and, during power plays, to be there when Nishikawa's lost somewhere up the ice trying to score one of his "glory" goals. The second is to help Sarah put him in his place when he's off the ice – since not even Muck can keep him in it when he's on the ice.

I love the Owls. I came to Tamarack from Winnipeg when my mother got a job teaching grade two at Lord Stanley Public School and my dad decided he'd always wanted a change and quit his job in the insurance office. He is still looking for something new to do. We love it here. There's plenty of snow in the winter and it doesn't blow into huge drifts the way it does in Manitoba. And while there's bugs in summer, they're nothing compared to what we had in Winnipeg. My dad always says Winnipeg mosquitoes are "Vampire" mosquitoes and it doesn't do any good to slap them – what you have to do is catch them, tie them down, and drive a stake through their heart!

SCOUTING REPORT

POS.	GAMES	GOALS	ASSISTS	POINTS	PIM
D	14	6	15	21	19

"Big and strong, Bennett is a truly dependable defender, always in position, always giving everything she has. Keeps the bench loose with her humour, too."

SAMANTHA BENNETT #4

But I do miss Winnipeg. I miss my friends and my neighbourhood and I miss going up to the lake, even though there's plenty of lakes here. And most of all I miss all those outdoor rinks, which is pretty well where I learned my hockey.

My dad's a hockey nut. He can tell you every single player on the 1970–71 Chicago Blackhawks. He can recite every team that ever won the Stanley Cup, in order, the way some people can recite poetry. He has a Bobby Hull rookie card – framed and signed – on the wall of his little office at home. He watches every game on television, listens on the radio when he can't find one on television, and stays up half the night watching the highlights from the games being played around the league. He's crazy and he made me crazy, too. I love him for it.

There's two girls in our family. Me and my older sister, Trish. I think my dad always dreamed of having a boy he could coach, but now I'm not so sure. We came along just as girls' hockey was taking off in Winnipeg and he signed up as a coach and all three of us started spending just about every single spare minute on the ice. He's a great coach. I hope someday he gets a chance to help Muck behind the bench. He says girls' hockey is actually superior, because girls have a better sense of team and are far more generous with the puck than most boys, who only think of themselves and their personal stats. Are you reading this, Nish?

Which brings me to my new best friend, Sarah Cuthbertson. Let me tell you, the last thing in the world I expected when my dad told me there was a good peewee team in town was that the best player on the team would turn out to be a girl! Maybe I'm being sexist, but any girl who plays this game knows what I mean. Boys have about a full century's head start on us. And they get the best coaching and the best ice time and everybody pays special attention to them, don't they? So it only stands to reason that I'd expect the top player to be a boy.

I made the team on account of a boy, Data, who got hurt. He's still with the Owls, though, and is just about my second-best friend on earth. We sometimes even try and speak Klingon together, but no way am I as good at it or as smart at computers as Data is. I just wish I'd been able to see him play. They say he was really good. Like me, he had the nasty task of cleaning up the messes Nish left on the ice. No one, by the way, has to clean up the messes he makes *off* the ice. I pity his poor mother.

But back to Sarah. I've never seen anyone quite like her. She skates almost as if she's moving through air, like she's in a space capsule somewhere and there's no gravity and all she has to do is push off with her baby finger and she's flying. She skates beautifully, she stickhandles so softly you can't even hear the puck on her stick, she passes brilliantly – all girls do, of course – and she can fire the puck as hard as any of them. Nish would claim he has the hardest shot on the team, and maybe he does, too, but I'm never going to admit it.

The one thing I do have over Sarah is strength. I can't explain it, but I'm probably the strongest player on the team. Nish says he's strongest – but we're not counting smell, are we? My dad says it has to do with my heritage. Three of my grandparents are Irish, and I have red hair I used to hate but now kind of like. He says it makes me "fiery" – like some sort of female warrior or something. All I know is that it gives me fair skin and I sunburn easily.

Another feature I have is a big mouth. Not big like in the mirror, but big as in LOUD. I like to yell. As a matter of fact, about the only thing I kind of admire in Nishikawa is his ability to let go a great yell every now and then. I think he secretly hates it that I do the "KA-WA-BUNG-GA!" better than him.

My big mouth can get me in trouble sometimes. I say things before I really mean to, and I know that can hurt people's feelings. That's the last thing in the world I intend to do. I just mean to be funny, but sometimes what seems like a smart thing to say turns out to sound mean when it was never meant to. I'm working on that. I'm also trying not to do stupid things when I know perfectly well I shouldn't. The thing is, I try to act tough when, in fact, I'm a softie inside. I'm not ashamed of being emotional – why would anyone be? – but I don't like it when I get so wound up.

We have unbelievable fun on the Owls. We get to travel and stay in neat places and we play against teams from all over the world – kids just like us who might not even speak our language but love hockey every bit as much as we do.

We even have our own special humour. Late at night, when we're back in our hotel, sometimes we girls get laughing so hard about something that happened out on the ice we start crying. Like the time that big toughie in Ottawa says to me that I better back off or he'll "take me out." And I say to him, "Are you asking me on a date?" I don't know who turned redder, him or me.

But the reddest I ever saw anyone turn was dear old Nishikawa in New York City when we went over to Rockefeller Center to skate on the outdoor

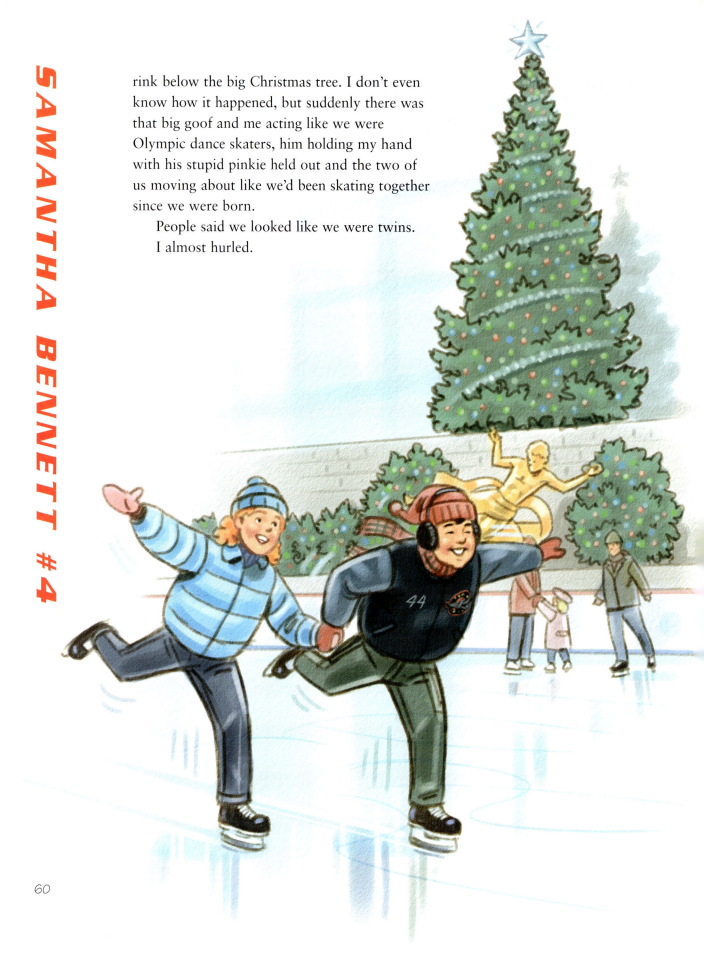

rink below the big Christmas tree. I don't even know how it happened, but suddenly there was that big goof and me acting like we were Olympic dance skaters, him holding my hand with his stupid pinkie held out and the two of us moving about like we'd been skating together since we were born.

People said we looked like we were twins.

I almost hurled.

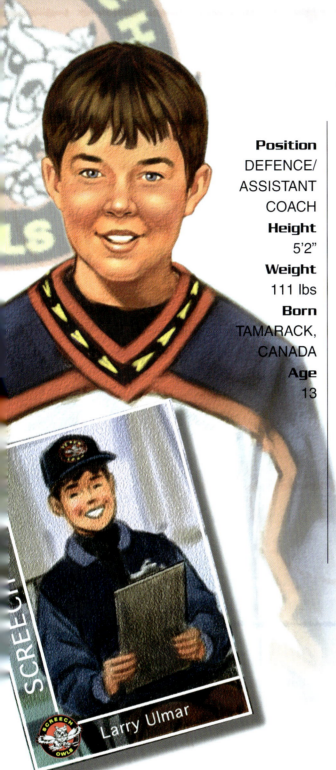

LARRY ULMAR #6

PLAYER PROFILE

Position
DEFENCE/
ASSISTANT
COACH

Height
5'2"

Weight
111 lbs

Born
TAMARACK,
CANADA

Age
13

Tlhlngan Hol Dajatlh'a'?

I didn't think so.

I asked if you speak Klingon, but the only other person I've ever met who even speaks just a bit of it is Samantha Bennett. Sometimes that's good – Sam and I can talk about Nish's stink ("*pIw*" in Klingon) without anyone knowing what we're laughing at – but sometimes it's not so good. I wouldn't mind meeting another kid more like me.

My real name's Larry Ulmar, but everyone calls me Data. It's partly because of me loving all those old space shows like *Star Trek* and *Star Wars*, but more and more lately it's been because I'm really into computers. Get it? Data – the computer nerd.

I used to be Nish's defence partner. More accurately, I was the one who cleaned up after him. If Nish decided he was going to carry the puck end-to-end, lose it, and then be too tired to come back and check the other team, I was always the one defenceman sure to be back. Good ol' dependable Data.

Everyone knows what happened. We were all hitching rides on back bumpers during a snow storm and this one car went out of control and hit Nish and me and I ended up in the hospital with a broken neck and about a 30-per-cent chance of survival.

SCOUTING REPORT

POS.	GAMES	GOALS	ASSISTS	POINTS	PIM
D	30	6	21	27	12

"Ulmar was a top defenceman for the Owls before his accident. Now serves as assistant coach and resident computer genius (with Noorizadeh). The heart and soul of the Screech Owls."

LARRY ULMAR #6

Well, I survived, obviously. I have a new wheelchair that I can drive almost anywhere. My parents fixed the house so that there's a ramp and I can get around inside without much worry. My two brothers have been great about it and help me as much as I want, whenever I want. We have a special van that can pick me up and deliver me somewhere or bring me home. And the school has been great. I get to use the freight elevator to go up to the library on the second floor. In fact, I'm the only kid in Lord Stanley Public School allowed on it – me and whoever I pick to come along with me, so I'm pretty popular around the school. Especially with Nish, who's too lazy to walk up a flight of stairs. He claims heights make him dizzy. He's dizzy all right.

Of course I don't like it. But I do most of my swearing in Klingon. Want to know some real dirty phrases in Klingon? Try this around your parents – "*QI'yah*" or "*ghuy'cha'*" – and see if you get a reaction. If they knew what you were saying, you'd be shut up in your room for a week!

But what's the point of being mad all the time? It was an accident. The drunk who hit me paid a price – lost his licence, got a huge fine, and spent weekends in jail for a month or so – but hardly a price equal to what he did to me. Maybe drunk drivers should have to spend a few years getting around in a wheelchair – or lie in a coffin for a couple of decades – so they'd get the message. But as I say, what's the point of being angry? What I do is make the best of it and believe that one day doctors are going to figure out how to fix spinal cords as well as broken bones and worn-out hearts. I plan to be there when that day comes.

In the meantime, I'm busier now than ever. I have my own Web site, and I have a big one up for the Screech Owls hockey team. Computers have become a really big thing with me, and I think when I grow up I'll be working with them. It's made me and Fahd much better friends now than we ever were before. I guess we're the two geeks on the team, but really, no one ever laughs at us. After all, if it wasn't for us sleuthing around on the computers, we might not have solved most of the crimes the Owls have run into.

Now I'm the Owls' assistant coach. It was Muck's idea. He called up to ask my parents about it and my mom started crying right on the phone.

Muck's been great. He's the one who brought me out of the hospital to that charity game where they raised the money for all the stuff I'd be needing. He's the one who got Paul Henderson and all those former NHLers to come and play against the Flying Fathers. And Mr. Dillinger's been super, too. He's the one who made sure my number 6 was "retired," and he's the guy who made up that little four-leaf clover with the "6" inside it and stitched it on all the jerseys. They're the most wonderful guys, you know. They make sure I'm at every game and that there's always a place for me to be with them behind the bench.

I can't say I do much. I hand around the water bottles and toss the odd towel. Most of my work on the team, however, is no different than when I actually played for them.

I just scream as loud as I can at Nish.

"Stay back!"

"Stay in position!"

"Stay with your check!"

"*Qu'vatlh!*"

That's Klingon for "#*@!"

I yell that a lot at Nish.

SIMON MILLIKEN #33

PLAYER PROFILE

Position
LEFT WING
Height
4'11"
Weight
99 lbs
Shoots
RIGHT
Born
MONTREAL, CANADA
Age
12

This is a funny team. I tell people it's tougher on the bus than it is on the ice. On the ice they judge you by your abilities. Off the ice, they judge everything: your personality, your family, your clothes, your size!

I had a rough time when I joined. I'm the only player who wears glasses (not when I actually play, though), and then Nish made this ridiculous rhyme on my name – "Chicken Milliken."

That's a bit unfair, considering the only evidence they had that I was afraid of anything was that I was small. As if people shrink when they're scared.

Well, it made me mad, and I guess it made me want to prove I'm not a chicken, which I did soon enough.

Since then, it's been great. Nish is off my case and the rest of the team is wonderful. Sarah Cuthbertson has become a great friend and she hardly needs any more friends. She's probably the most popular player on the team. And Travis and I are becoming pretty close, too.

I don't know what I'll be when I grow up. Part of me never wants to grow up. And another part of me can hardly wait to grow up so I'll stop being the smallest kid on the team.

What I need is someone to do for me what I did for Travis. Until I got here, he was the little one. I need my own Little Simon Milliken to show up.

Either that or else someone to puncture Nish so he shrivels up and shrinks!

SCOUTING REPORT

POS.	GAMES	GOALS	ASSISTS	POINTS	PIM
F	14	8	11	19	6

"Little Milliken gets called 'Chicken' sometimes, but he's a courageous little player on the ice. If the Owls desperately need a goal, he's often the one to surprise."

"Stay in Position"

"Okay," Muck said. Instantly the room went silent. Muck never had to raise his voice, that's how much respect the players had for their coach.

"This is a team we haven't seen before. I don't expect they're going to give us too much trouble, but by the same token I don't expect us to do anything but play our game. That means what, Nish?"

Nish had been staring down between his knees, concentrating.

"'Stay in position,'" Nish quoted. It was one of Muck's favourite phrases, and Nish almost sounded like the coach when he said it. Travis knew why Muck had asked Nish; everyone knew who the worst offender was if a game was too easy. Nish would suddenly think he was Paul Coffey, rushing end to end with the puck.

"That's right," agreed Muck. "Stay in position. No dumb moves. No 'glory hogs.'"

Nish looked up abruptly, surprised that Muck would use the same expression his teammates used when they were ragging on him. Muck stared right back, a small grin at the corners of his mouth.

"I want to see passing. I want to see you use your points. I want to see everyone – and I mean everyone – coming back to help out your defence and goaltender.

"Now let's go."

(from *The Night They Stole the Stanley Cup*)

"Never Humiliate an Opponent"

It was clear by the end of the first period that the team from Hanna was badly outclassed by the Owls. Instinctively, the Owls began to hold back a bit, knowing that Muck never, ever wanted them to run up the score on a team. "Never humiliate an opponent," he used to say. "You try to embarrass the team you're playing against, you really just embarrass yourself."

(from *Danger in Dinosaur Valley*)

"New Equipment Won't Improve Your Game"

"The one thing in hockey you can't buy is skill."

Muck hated to see a kid come out with a brand-new pair of gloves – "You may as well dip your hands in wet cement," he'd say – and told them all that top-of-the-line skates were a waste of money for players who were still growing. "What's it matter if you start the season with an extra pair of socks and end it in your bare feet?" he'd ask. "Bobby Orr never wore socks in his skates – and he was the best skater there ever was."

(from *Terror in Florida*)

"Use Your Speed"

The Wheels were bigger than the Owls. They were bigger and stronger and played a more physical game. First shift out, Nish got hammered into a corner on a play that Mr. Dillinger shouted should have been a penalty. No penalty was called, and Nish got right back up and into the game. No grandstanding.

"We're faster," Muck said after the first few shifts. "We can get a step on them. Speed is still the most intimidating thing in hockey – don't forget that when you're out there."

(From *Sudden Death in New York City*)

"Over-ambitious Parents"

Muck quickly fixed Mr. Brown with the stare his players seldom saw and, once seen, never wished to see again. The stare of a laser beam burning through steel.

Muck was looking at Mr. Brown but speaking to everyone: "I have been around this coaching business long enough to know that sometimes we can all let a simple game matter a bit too much and, before we know it, we've made fools of ourselves without even realizing what we were doing. There are some fathers – and some mothers – in this very room who know what I'm talking about. Ripping the head off some thirteen-year-old referee. Swearing at some little kid just because he happened to run into yours. Yelling at your own kid after a game because he missed a pass."

"That's hardly the same thing –" protested Mr. Brown.

Muck's stare turned into a hard drive from the point, labelled.

"I've even heard of grown-ups offering bribes to children," Muck said. "You don't get much lower than that in my book."

(from *Mystery at Lake Placid*)

Borje Salming's Coaching Tips

Salming scooped up the puck with his stick. He did it the way Travis had seen other NHLers do it. Effortlessly, smoothly, the stick snaked out, snaked back, and, as if by magic, the puck was suddenly lying on the blade and then floating through the air until it landed, perfectly, in the palm of his glove. He didn't seem to be even thinking about it.

Salming held up the puck. "I don't have to tell you that the game is all about this and what you are able to do with it," he said. "But we want to show you how kids learn the game in Sweden."

He reached into his track-suit pocket, removed another puck, and held it up beside the puck he had scooped from the ice. This one was different. It was about half the size.

"We teach Swedish youngsters how to handle small pucks first," he said.

"You don't give a full-size basketball to a five-year-old, do you? No matter how tall he is."

"No," Fahd said. Fahd could always be counted on to say the obvious.

"The game in Europe is all about tempo," Salming said. "Anyone know what I mean by 'tempo'? Anyone a musician?"

Fahd, of course, raised his hand. "I play piano."

"Well?"

"Tempo tells you how slow or fast to play the piece of music."

Salming smiled, nodding. "Same in hockey. If you can learn to do drills at full speed, then you won't even have to think about what you should be doing during a game. Little kids can't handle NHL regulation pucks the

same way they can these little things. And obviously they can't shoot them the same."

He pointed to four red frames the other coaches had set up. They faced each other in two pairs on each side of the centre red line.

"Little pucks require little nets," he said, indicating the frames. "We teach our skills this way. Young players can handle these little pucks better, and shoot them a lot better. We use the smaller nets to teach accuracy."

Salming divided the Owls into two groups, one for the pair of tiny nets at the far end of the Globen rink, one for the near end. The rules were simple: no offsides, no stoppages, be creative, take chances.

Travis had never heard such talk from a coach – not even Muck, who believed in having fun on the ice and almost always gave them a few minutes of shinny at the end of a practice. But even when they played shinny back in Canada there would be whistles, and play would be stopped, and coaches would explain mistakes. Here there would be nothing. No control. No teaching. No stopping. Nothing.

In all his hockey years, Travis had never experienced anything quite like this. It was wonderful. It was exciting. It was fun – more fun, he thought, than he had ever had on an ice surface.

They played in groups of three: Travis, Dmitri, and Sarah against Nish, Data, and big Andy Higgins. Borje Salming and the other coach at their end just threw the puck into the corner and the game was under way. All four coaches then formed a line across centre to stop the little pucks from crossing the centre line.

The pucks felt almost weightless. Travis found he could stickhandle like an NHL pro. And when he shot, it took the slightest flick of his wrist to send a snap shot hard and high off the glass. He couldn't believe it! And yet there was no point in pounding a shot off the glass just because it sounded great. As he played and sweated and gasped for breath, Travis realized that this explained everything he had ever wondered about European hockey.

Here, on half the ice in the Globen Arena in Stockholm, with a baby puck and a toy net, he could see it all for the first time: the only way that he and Dmitri and Sarah could attack was to keep circling back and dropping the puck to each other, even if they had only half the ice surface to work with. They had to drop the puck and watch for either Nish or Data or Andy to commit themselves, allowing them a quick three-on-two. The puck was so small and light that they could pass it back and forth effortlessly and quickly, and the passing became almost hypnotic as they kept trying out new ideas. They could do anything they wanted – no whistles, no one yelling at them, no score to worry about. They circled and dropped and flicked quick little passes and kept the puck dancing on the ends of their sticks.

Scoring, however, was another matter. The net was so small that, with Nish and his big shin pads in the way, it was a bit like threading a needle. If they kept to the usual North American strategy they would lose possession. A shot wasn't always a safe play. Here, a shot for the sake of a shot was a waste. They had to wait, and they had to work at it so one

of them would have the ideal angle. No big fancy slapshots. Quick, hard shots exactly placed – nothing else would work.

They played for nearly half an hour, and when Salming finally blew the whistle and the other coaches began to gather up the little pucks and push away the tiny nets, the Owls collapsed on their backs, sweating and puffing and giggling.

"That's *my* kind of hockey," Dmitri said.

"I *love* it!" said Sarah.

(from *Kidnapped in Sweden*)

JESSE HIGHBOY #10

PLAYER PROFILE

Position
RIGHT WING

Height
5'4"

Weight
126 lb

Shoots
RIGHT

Born
WASKAGANISH, CANADA

Age
13

I come from Waskaganish, a tiny little village in the north on the shores of James Bay. My family is Cree. My grandparents still live most of their year out in the bush on a trap line that my granddad's father and his grandfather before him ran. And when they're not on the trap line they're in the camps hunting the geese that fly south in the late fall and back up north in the spring. They live entirely off the land. Sometimes we eat seal flippers, sometimes beaver, sometimes even my good friend Nish's all-time favourite meal – moose nostrils!

I like being different. We're only going to be living in Tamarack for a few years while my father completes this contract he's working on, and then we'll go back to Waskaganish. But a part of me will always be here with the Owls. It's been the greatest experience of my life playing for them. I'm not very good, but I don't mind saying there's no one on the team who tries harder than I do.

The best was when we took the team up to Cree Country. It was like they'd gone to another planet. But it was great. They got to meet all the kids in my village – I don't think Travis will ever get over my cousin, Rachel – and some of them even got to go out to my grandparents' cabin in the wood and meet them.

SCOUTING REPORT

POS.	GAMES	GOALS	ASSISTS	POINTS	PIM
F	43	16	12	28	11

"Jesse is working on his speed and shot, but he's already got fantastic hockey sense. On an outdoor rink, he can rule."

JESSE HIGHBOY #10

Nish almost died on that trip. His snowmobile went through the ice and we had to pull him out and build a fire and spend a night out in the freezing cold with no protection. I'm just so glad Rachel was with us. We were able to build a shelter out of spruce boughs and a got a good fire going and, I guess it's okay to say, we probably saved Nish's life.

Then my grandfather found us and took us ahead to the cabin, and after that we played the Biggest Outdoor Hockey Game in History, with all of frozen James Bay for us to skate on. My grandfather even came out and played – with a shovel for a goalie stick!

After that, I think I had new respect on the team.

Thank you, Grandfather – for everything.

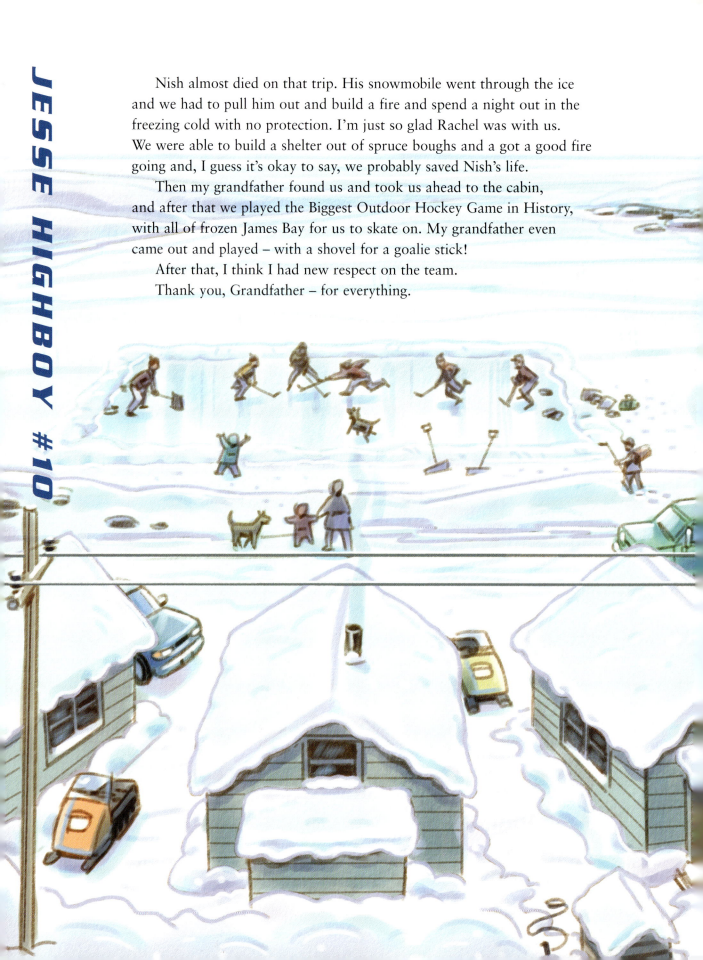

LIZ MOSCOVITZ #21

PLAYER PROFILE

Position
LEFT WING
Height
5'3"
Weight
102 lbs
Shoots
LEFT
Born
VICTORIA, CANADA
Age
13

Hi, I'm Liz – third-line winger on the Screech Owls. I'm no Sarah Cuthbertson, but I'm quite content with what's happening with my hockey, thank you.

My mom thinks I'm crazy to play. She wanted me to stick to ringette, which is a fine game, but I wanted real hockey competition and I wanted a way to get better as a hockey player – and there's only the one way to do that, the way I see it.

I may not be the best player, but I'm the most stubborn. Just ask my teachers what I'm like. Some of them would probably love it if I switched schools and got out of their hair, but I'm just watching out for myself. I'm not too big, and I'm not too noticeable, but I'll be darned if I'm going to be ignored.

My dad thinks it's funny. He says with my personality I'm going somewhere. He says he wouldn't be surprised to see me prime minister one day.

Maybe I will be. All I know for sure is Liz Moscovitz is going to be somebody some day.

Maybe I'm third line right now, but not for long. Remember the number – 21.

You haven't seen the last of it.

SCOUTING REPORT

POS.	GAMES	GOALS	ASSISTS	POINTS	PIM
F	43	11	11	22	5

"Quick, peppy winger who tries her heart out every game. A little more size and Moscovitz will be a force in this league."

DMITRI YAKUSHEV #91

PLAYER PROFILE

Position
RIGHT WING

Height
5'5"

Weight
134 lbs

Shoots
RIGHT

Born
LENINGRAD, RUSSIA

Age
13

The rest of the team likes to kid me about not talking too much. I can't help it. It's the way I am. A lot of Russians are that way.

I was born in Leningrad, which used to be called St. Petersburg and is now back to being called St. Petersburg. It's where the Russian Revolution began, way back in 1917. I was born there after what my family calls the *second* Russian Revolution put an end to the old Soviet Union. If that hadn't happened, my family would never have been able to leave. My parents had been wanting to come to Canada for years and years. Not that they don't love Russia – they do – but they wanted us to have a new life here. It was the best thing that ever happened to me.

The second best thing was joining the Screech Owls. My father had played in Moscow – his cousin is Alexander Yakushev, who was the leading scorer for the Soviets in the famous 1972 Summit Series – and then he played in Leningrad when he was working in the shipyards there. He was a pretty fair hockey player, and maybe if he'd been a bit younger and come to Canada sooner, he might have had a chance to play professional hockey in North America. He taught me how to skate and most of what I know about hockey. He doesn't push me much, and though he complained about every coach I had all through initiation and mite and atom, once I got to play for Muck Munro my father backed right off. In fact, he's Muck's best supporter. He says Muck doesn't wear blindfolds like most coaches – but I'm not sure what he means by that.

I play on a line with Travis and Sarah. Sarah's the centre and makes most of the plays. Travis is really good at reading Sarah and good at digging the puck out and getting it to one of us. They both tell

SCOUTING REPORT

POS.	GAMES	GOALS	ASSISTS	POINTS	PIM
F	43	53	19	72	2

"The Owls' very own 'Russian Rocket' – Yakushev is so fast it sometimes looks like he's going to leave his skates! Perfect winger for Cuthbertson, who can find him breaking in any crowd. His backhand water-bottle-off-the-back-of-the-net shot is becoming legendary."

me just to "Go!" and if I'm clear, they'll get me the puck. I score a lot of my goals on breakaways.

My dream is simple: to play for as long as I can for the Owls, on the same line as Sarah and Travis, and then one day to get drafted into the NHL so I can live out my father's great dream, even if he won't admit it.

Oh yeah, and to win a Stanley Cup by scoring the overtime goal in Game Seven. On a breakaway, of course, with a quick fake to the backhand and a high, hard shot that knocks the water bottle off the back of the net!

"Wedgie Stop!"

"WEDGIE STOP!"

"WEDDD-GEEE stop!"

Mr. Dillinger was still shouting and laughing as he put the old bus in park and hopped out onto the shoulder of the road. He ran around to the front of the bus, bending over and wiggling so his big belly rippled right through his shirt, and with his hands pulling at the seat of his pants, he pretended to be yanking a huge "wedgie" of bunched-up underwear out of his rear end.

Howling with laughter, the team followed suit, a dozen young players out on the side of the road yanking at their pants to free up their underwear and wiggling their rear ends at the other cars that roared by, the drivers and passengers either staring out as if the Screech Owls should be arrested or else pretending the Screech Owls were not even there, a dozen youngsters at the side of the road, bent over, with a hand on each side of their pants, pulling wedgies.

"All 'board!" Mr. Dillinger hollered as he jumped in the van. The team scrambled back in, Nish and several others laughing so hard they had tears in their eyes.

Mr. Dillinger started up the van, then turned, his face unsmiling, voice as serious as a vice principal's.

"The United States of America takes wedgies very seriously," he announced. "At the border they will ask you where you were born and whether or not you are having any difficulty with your underwear. If they suspect you are having problems, you will be body-searched. If they find any wedgies, you will spend the rest of your life . . ."

He paused, waiting.

Nish finished for him: ". . . in prison?"

Mr. Dillinger stared, then smiled: "In Pampers, Nish, in Pampers."

(from *Mystery at Lake Placid*)

"A Head Full of Shaving Cream"

"PIT STOP!"

Travis jumped. He had been dozing again. His head felt thick, his eyes out of focus. He rubbed them as Mr. Dillinger called again from the driver's seat of the bus.

"Pit Stop! Last one before Lake Placid! Ten minutes! You go now or you go later in your pants – this means you, Nish!"

Travis could hear them giggling. His vision cleared and he saw that everyone in the van was looking back at him. Because he had fallen asleep, obviously. Well, so what? But they wouldn't stop laughing.

"What's so funny?" Travis asked Nish, who had turned around, his face looking like it was about to split.

"Mr. Dillinger. Didn't you hear him?"

It didn't make sense, but Travis let it go. He headed into the restaurant, pushed the door open, saw that everyone in there was laughing at the team coming in – what was the matter with them, never see hockey players in a bus? – and decided that he'd better go to the washroom first.

Funny, there was no line-up. Nish and some of the other kids were hanging around outside the door but they didn't seem to want to go in. More like they were waiting. Travis pushed past them through the door, turned to the mirror – and saw immediately what his teammates, and all the people in the restaurant, had been giggling at.

HIS HEAD WAS COVERED IN CREAM!

It had been put on like a cone. Swirled like he was about to be dipped into chocolate at Dairy Queen. He looked like a fool. But it was so light he hadn't felt it. That's why they'd been laughing at him. It was hilariously obvious to everyone but Travis himself, who couldn't even feel it up there.

Travis grabbed a handful of the cream and threw it off his head into the sink. He reached for some paper towels and began rubbing it off. On the other side of the door, he could hear the entire team howling with laughter as they imagined his reaction.

Travis smelled his hands. Shaving cream. There was only one person in the Screech Owls van old enough to shave.

Mr. Dillinger.

(from *Mystery at Lake Placid*)

"Frozen Underwear"

"WHO TOOK MY UNDERWEAR?"

Travis had never heard such a ridiculous question. Nish was still in his pyjamas while everyone else was dressed and ready to head off for the first game of the Little Stanley Cup. They had ten minutes to be in the hotel lobby – and Nish hadn't even brushed his teeth yet.

"Somebody took my underwear. Come on, now! This is ridiculous!"

I'll say it is, thought Travis. Ridiculous that Nish could be thirteen years old and still not know how to pack for a road trip. He had already emptied the entire contents of his suitcase out on the bed he and Travis were sharing and ploughed through his clothes like a dog rooting through garbage. Enough T-shirts to supply the team – each one proof that he had played in hockey tournaments everywhere from Lake Placid to Quebec City – pants and sweatshirts and socks and comic books and deodorant and toothpaste and toothbrush – but no underwear. He'd only brought the pair he was wearing, and now he couldn't even find them!

"This is a SICK joke!" Nish said. He was getting upset.

"*You're* a sick joke," said Willie Granger. Willie was sharing the other bed with Data, Nish's defence partner. "You can't even pack a suitcase."

"You should have had your mom do it," said Data, who was growing a bit anxious about the deadline for being in the lobby.

Nish held up his hands. "Stop! Just sit on it, okay? We know they were here last night."

"*You* know they were here last night," corrected Willie.

"Who else was here?"

"Who wasn't here?" said Travis. He was right. Their room had been like a bus terminal. Everyone had run down after they checked in to see the four who'd lucked into a suite when the hotel ran out of regular rooms. There was a bedroom off a sitting room, two televisions, and a small kitchen with a refrigerator. Everyone had jealously checked out everything in the suite, but surely not Nish's underwear.

"Okay!" Nish shouted. He was beginning to panic. "We know they're here *somewhere*."

"I'm not touching your shorts!" Data shouted back.

"No one's asking you to *touch* them – just *point* when you find them!" Nish said. He was getting testy. "Travis and Data, you two do the other room and kitchen. Willie will help me do the bathroom and bedroom. Look absolutely everywhere – and *hurry!*"

They didn't like doing it, but what choice did they have? Nish had to have underwear, and he was far too big and heavy to wear anyone else's. So they began looking, Nish and Willie taking the bedroom apart bit by bit, and Travis and Data going over the sitting room and the kitchen.

"You look in the kitchen cupboards," Data said. "I'll check in here behind all the cushions."

"We didn't use the cupboards," Travis said.

"Maybe someone threw them there as a joke."

Unconvinced, Travis began looking. He checked each cupboard – nothing. He checked all the drawers – no underwear.

The only thing left to check was the refrigerator. Surely, no. He opened the door – no luck. He flicked open the freezer compartment. There was something inside. Whatever it was, it was crumpled up and covered with frost. He poked at it. It was as hard as a rock. Then he recognized the blue diamond pattern of Nish's boxer shorts.

"*They're here!*" Travis called out.

Nish came running into the room, already dropping his pyjamas. "*Gimme them!*"

"You'll have to *chip* them out," said Travis.

Nish stopped dead in his tracks, his eyes big as hockey pucks.

"*What kind of a sick joke is this!*" he shouted.

He pulled at the shorts and they cracked, frozen. He pulled again and they gave. He began unfolding them, the frost drifting in the air as they bent in his hands.

"*Who* would do this?"

"Not me."

"Wasn't me."

"I never."

It wasn't any of them, either. They all knew that. Who'd have the guts to touch Nish's shorts in the first place?

"This isn't fair," Nish wailed. "I got nothing else to wear!"

"Then you've got no choice, do you?" Data said. "We gotta roll – and quick."

The others went down to the lobby ahead of Nish. Muck was already there, checking his watch. The rest of the team and some of the parents were standing around and waiting as well.

"Where's Nishikawa?" Muck asked.

"He's coming," said Travis.

Everyone waited. Finally the elevator doors opened, and out walked Nish, his face in agony, his steps uncertain.

"What's with him?" Muck asked. "Got cold feet over the tournament?"

"Not exactly," Travis answered.

(from *The Night They Stole the Stanley Cup*)

"Prehistoric Dung"

"There's so much we don't know," said the guide. "Before 1824 they didn't even know dinosaurs once existed. We don't know whether they were cold- or warm-blooded. We don't know what colour they were. We don't even know what they sounded like."

"Did they fart?" a small voice squeaked from the back.

"Excuse me?" the guide said, trying to see who had spoken.

No one spoke. Travis cringed, knowing at once who it was.

"You said something, young man?" the guide said pointedly to Nish.

"N-no," Nish mumbled.

"I didn't think so," the guide said. "If you have something to say, please tell us all, though, will you?"

"O . . . kay," Nish mumbled even lower.

"*Ontariosaurus*," Sarah said. Everyone, the guide included, laughed.

"Actually, young man, we do have something over here you might be interested in."

They crossed to a special display, and the guide stopped in front of what appeared to be a polished rock.

"Any idea what this might be, young man?" the guide asked Nish.

Nish looked, his eyes squinting with suspicion. "N-no."

"It's *coprolites*. Anyone have any idea what that means?"

The guide looked around. Data was raising his hand.

"Yes?" the guide asked.

"It's dung, isn't it?"

The guide's eyes lighted up. "Good for you. Yes, dung. Prehistoric poop. This one's probably twenty million years old."

"Does it still smell?" Nish asked.

"A smell wouldn't last twenty million years, young man," the guide said, shaking his head.

"You obviously haven't spent much time around Nish," Wilson said, breaking up the group.

(from *Danger in Dinosaur Valley*)

"A Special Swedish Treat"

The Screech Owls hadn't played a single game in Sweden, and already this was the best tournament ever. After the practice, the lumber company Lars's father worked for was treating them to a banquet in the restaurant overlooking the ice surface, high up on the seventh floor of the Globen Arena complex. But the Owls kept forgetting they had come up here to eat. MoDo, one of the Swedish elite teams, was holding a practice below for their upcoming game against Djurgårdens.

"They're playing with little pucks like the ones we used in practice!" Fahd shouted.

"They just *look* little from up here," said Travis, shaking his head at Fahd.

The meal included delicious tiny boiled potatoes and lots of different kinds of cheese. Lars wanted them all to try the pickled herring, but he couldn't convince them that the herring wasn't a snake all curled up in the dish.

"Let me at it!" shouted Nish from another table.

Ever since the trip to James Bay, Nish fancied himself a new Man of the World. He had eaten beaver, after all – and *moose nostrils*! – so what was the big deal about a little slippery, rubbery fish?

"You eat this, Nish," Lars said, "and you get first dibs on the pudding."

Nish's eyes opened wide. "What pudding?"

"A special Swedish treat. You can go first if you eat this."

"*No prob-lem*," Nish announced, as he sat down and elaborately tucked a napkin under his chin.

He sliced off a bit of the pickled herring, sniffed it, and began to chew.

"*Mmmmmmm*," he kept saying. "*Ahhhhhhh! Per-fect!*"

Nish chewed and ate as if he'd been brought up on nothing but pickled herring. He loved a show. He loved being the centre of attention.

"You win!" said Lars. "Bring Nish some of the pudding."

Nish put down his knife and fork and dabbed at his chin, waiting, like some ancient king on his throne, for someone to serve him.

A smiling waiter came over with the special dish Lars has promised.

Nish lightly dabbed at his mouth. "I should have some wine to clean my palate," he announced grandly.

"*You're thirteen years old!*" Fahd scolded.

"There is no drinking age in Sweden," said Nish. "Is there, Lars?"

"Well, you have to be eighteen, actually," Lars said. "But it's pretty well left up to the parents to decide when you're mature enough – which in your case would be roughly the year 2036."

Nish scowled. "*Very* funny."

The waiter placed the pudding in front of Nish and stood back.

"*Lemme at it!*" Nish practically shouted.

"Go ahead," Lars said. "You've earned it."

Nish didn't even bother to sniff the dish. Like a front-end loader dumping snow into the back of a truck, he spooned up pudding, chewed once with his eyes closed – then stopped, his eyes opening wide!

"W-what *is* this?" he mumbled, some of the dark pudding tumbling out of his mouth.

"The English translation," said Lars, "would be 'blood pudding.' There's beer and syrup and spices mixed together with flour." He paused, grinning. "Oh yes, and the blood of a freshly slaughtered pig. It's a very

old, very special Swedish recipe. It dates back hundreds and hundreds of years."

More of the dark pudding rolled out of Nish's open mouth. He turned pale.

"I THINK I'M GONNA HU-URLLL!"

(from *Kidnapped in Sweden*)

"In Full Equipment"

Travis thought to himself: *It's a good thing that we're capturing this on film, otherwise no one would ever believe it!*

They were deep in the bush behind the garbage dump. They knew they were in the right area when Jesse found a large beech tree with sharp, regularly spaced scrapings across the bark.

"A bear has scratched here to sharpen his claws," he announced.

Travis looked up, way up. For a bear to reach that high, it would have to be twice the height of Travis. At least. He shuddered.

"*What's this?*" Nish called from farther up the trail.

The others hurried along. Nish was standing over a huge black mound of what looked, on first glance, like mud

"Bear dropping," said Jesse.

Nish giggled. "How come we don't call it 'dropping'?"

"Because most of us have the decency to use a toilet," said Sam.

"At least this proves a bear has been here recently," said Simon.

"Time to get ready, Stinker Boy," said Sarah.

All eyes were now on Nish. He was already sweating. His face was twisted like an old sock.

"We're *not* going to do this," he wailed.

"We are so." said Sam. "Now get your stuff on!"

And that was how Wayne Nishikawa came to be walking down a bush trail in full lacrosse goalie equipment. He looked a bit like a bear himself, the heavy equipment nearly doubling his bulk and making him waddle as he walked.

Sam's idea had been ingenious, Travis thought. They needed a terrific, horrific smell that no bear on earth could help but notice.

What better than Nish's lacrosse equipment?

(from *Horror on River Road*)

"Wreck Beach Wrecked"

"*What the hell is that?*" howled Derek, staring in the direction of the glass front door.

The Screech Owls all turned at once. The door opened, wind and rain bursting in as if someone had turned a fire hose on the motel entrance.

And with the wind and rain came a strange wet creature. It put its back to the door, pushing hard to close it. The latch caught, shutting the storm outside, and the room filled with silence. Silence but for the huffing and puffing of the creature who had burst in.

It wore a soaked bucket hat that hung so limp over the creature's face they couldn't see its eyes. There was something white smeared down its nose and cheeks. There was an unbuttoned shirt, wet through and clinging like paint to the heaving chest of whatever was beneath it. There was a bathing suit, halfway down the creature's hips, heavy with water and threatening to drop. There was a dripping sports bag, a half-finished bottle of blue Gatorade sticking out past the dangling earphones of a portable CD.

"*Nish!*" Sam ventured.

Travis said nothing. He didn't need the creature to speak to know what it was.

The creature was shaking and shivering right in front of them. Its teeth were clicking together. It was moaning.

"*Where were you?*" Sarah asked.

The soaking wet bucket cap came off, revealing a very wet Wayne Nishikawa. He wiped the back of his arm across his face, smearing the white sunscreen from ear to ear.

"Nowhere," he mumbled through chattering teeth.

"You weren't looking for that nude beach, were you, Nish?" Sam demanded loudly.

Everyone started laughing.

"*None of your business!*" Nish practically spat.

"Whadya see, Nish," Andy teased, "bare-naked . . . ducks?"

Nish scowled in Andy's direction. He shook himself like a big dog and started to walk towards the corridor leading to his room. His sandals squished as he stepped, large, wet footprints mapping his progress. Nish paused at the doorway, peeled off his drenched shirt and shook it, spraying water in the Owls' direction without so much as turning around. His wet bathing suit had slipped down even further, his cheeks bulging above the elastic. He stuck his bum out, half-mooning the Owls.

"I'M GONNA HURL!" howled Sam.

(from *The West Coast Murders*)

DEREK DILLINGER #19

PLAYER PROFILE

Position
CENTRE
LEFT WING

Height
5'5"

Weight
142 lb

Shoots
LEFT

Born
TORONTO, CANADA

Age
13

It's tough being a kid on the team with your dad behind the bench. Most teams have a father coaching, but we're really lucky to have Muck doing that job. Muck has no family ties to any of us, so everyone knows that when he tells you something there's no other string pulling him.

My dad is the manager, the bus driver, the skate sharpener, the trainer, and the joker. The other kids adore him. I can't treat him quite the same as they do because he's . . . well, he's my dad.

I thought I'd have to quit the team after what happened in Lake Placid. My dad got way, way out of control there and did some very stupid things. I do give him credit, though. After he realized what he'd done – he thought it was for me! – he said he was sorry and was so sincere about it that Muck took him right back as team manager. It was a strange, strange week. I was ashamed of him one minute, proud of him the next. Maybe that's the way all kids are with their parents – but all kids aren't surrounded by a hockey team when they go through these things. It's tough, like I say.

Some of the Owls, like Travis, say I'm too serious. I guess I'm more like my mom, because I'm the total opposite of my dad. I'm all business out there. I love the physical side of the game, and the more we're allowed to hit, the happier I am.

I don't know what I'll be when I grow up. I'd like to keep playing, of course, but I also like science a lot and would like to be an engineer or an architect.

Maybe I'll change by then. Maybe if I have kids I'll let them have "Stupid Stops," too, but for the moment my dad and I are just too close for me to be any more like him than I am right now (I'm on the bench, he's right behind it). It's tough.

SCOUTING REPORT

POS.	GAMES	GOALS	ASSISTS	POINTS	PIM
F	43	23	20	43	17

"No one works harder than Dillinger. What he lacks in talent, he more than makes up for in try – the type of player teammates adore."

FAHD NOORIZADEH #12

PLAYER PROFILE

Position
DEFENCE/
RIGHT WING

Height
5'1"

Weight
103 lb

Shoots
RIGHT

Born
TORONTO,
CANADA

Age
12

Things have been a lot better for me since we went to British Columbia and played in that three-on-three tournament. I'm considered almost a "good" player now – just because in three-on-three lack of speed can sometimes be as useful as speed. I'm the King of the Pause, Lars says, and he says that knowing when to pause is the secret to winning those games.

I haven't the heart to tell Lars my problem is I can't *not* pause!

But Muck says everyone has a role to play on the team, and I know what mine is: just to be there. I'm defence, but I'm not very big. I am, however, excellent in mathematics, and I try to apply mathematical thinking to hockey. If Travis Lindsay thinks of a play, he must see all kinds of things happening and the puck carrier moving all over the place, twisting and turning for a chance. I see the game more like an engineer. What's the shortest route from point A to point B. I also try and think ahead. I read once where Wayne Gretzky said, "I try and skate to where the puck's going to be, not where it's been" – and that's exactly what I try to do.

I love playing for the Owls. All of them are great, and I don't really care how much fun Nish makes of me for asking what he calls "stupid questions." I ask questions I want answers to. Nish

SCOUTING REPORT

POS.	GAMES	GOALS	ASSISTS	POINTS	PIM
D/F	43	7	19	26	8

"Plays up or back. Not the world's fastest skater, but determined and game. Noorizadeh also has an uncanny ability to ask the obvious question."

is the kind of person who thinks he already has all the answers. We'll see who's ahead when we're both thirty.

I was born in Tamarack. My grandfather had a jewellery store along Main Street that my uncle now runs. My father is an investment counsellor and my mother is an accountant out at the chipboard plant, so she works for Lars's dad, who's a very nice person, she says. I have three sisters. None of them play hockey but all of them are busy with school and after-school activities. I like my family.

There's no NHL in my future. I'm not stupid, no matter how often Nish says it. I'm slim and my father's slim and my mother's very tiny. The chances of Fahd Noorizadeh, aged eighteen, five-foot-six, 135 pounds, being selected in the first round of the NHL entry draft six years from now are nil, absolutely nil. Maybe I'll be bigger, but not big enough.

Besides, I have other plans. Data and I are getting more and more into computers these days. We can do our own programming, and we already proved in New York that we can pretty well hack into anything we want any time we want. What we don't want is to go to jail, so we have to make sure we use our talents to do good things rather than bad.

No matter what that big butt says back on defence, I'm not stupid.

He might make the NHL, but I'll own the team.

GORDIE GRIFFITH #11

PLAYER PROFILE

Position CENTRE
Height 5'9"
Weight 140 lbs
Shoots RIGHT
Born HALIFAX, CANADA
Age 13

My family doctor says I'm just going through a growth spurt, but this is getting ridiculous!

I know Travis is worried about never growing. Maybe we could split this spurt and then we'd both be happy! I'm heading for six feet, with no sign of stopping!

My dad's big. And my mom's tall. And I've got an uncle who's six-foot-seven and used to play basketball. But I'm not convinced there's any great height advantage in hockey. The New York Islanders have that defenceman, Zdeno Chara, who's six-foot-nine – but I don't see him challenging Chris Pronger for the Norris Trophy or anything. I just hope I don't get too tall for the Owls.

Size is a funny thing in hockey. A lot of people assume if you're big then you're a hitter, or even a fighter, but I'm not nearly as physical out there as, say, Derek. And as for fighting, I've never been in a fight in my life. Unless you count pillow fights with my sister.

What I think I offer to the team is dependability. I'm not very fast, and I don't hit anyone, but I take my defensive play very seriously and I try to never, ever be caught out of position. I may be slow, but I'm pretty effective. And every team needs guys like me, I think.

I just hope I stop growing one of these days. I'm not the one trying to get in the *Guinness Book of World Records*. We all know who that is – and I'm about as opposite to him as it's possible to get!

SCOUTING REPORT

POS.	GAMES	GOALS	ASSISTS	POINTS	PIM
F	41	14	13	27	15

"Tall, tall, tall playmaker sometimes called 'Gordie Giraffe' by teammates – but takes it all in good sport. Can score the big goal when necessary."

A GALLERY OF UNFORGETTABLE VILLAINS

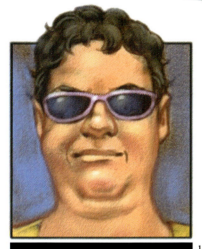

Buddy O'Reilly

Willie Granger, the Owls' trivia expert, said Buddy O'Reilly had played three NHL games for the Philadelphia Flyers – "No goals, no assists, no points, thirty-two minutes in penalties" – but he carried himself as if he'd won three Stanley Cups. Buddy had on shorts, a tank top, and thongs. He was also wearing neon-purple wraparound sun-glasses. And he was chewing gum, fast, using just his front teeth. He was holding a cellphone in his right hand, as if waiting for an important call, and had a whistle around his neck. His tank top had the logo of the hockey camp on the back and one word, *Coach*, stitched over his heart. He seemed to be laughing at Muck.

(from *Murder at Hockey Camp*)

A man was standing beside the Owls' bench. There was something about the cut of his suit and the look of him that told Travis he was Russian. The man was chewing on a toothpick, and when he worked his lips Travis could see the flash of a gold tooth. He looked nasty. But Travis supposed that was how a Russian undercover cop would look.

(from *Kidnapped in Sweden*)

Gold Tooth

The "Campers"

At the end of the path, two men were waiting. They both wore dark sunglasses. One, with his head shaved, wore army-style camouflage pants. The other, his dark hair tied back in a ponytail, wore a Chicago Bulls basketball jersey.

    They didn't look much like campers.

(from *Terror in Florida*)

Much to his surprise, Travis felt instantly at ease with the reporter. Bart Lundrigan was young, and he had a shock of dark curly hair that danced down into his eyes. He was wearing jeans and looked more like a movie star than a reporter.

(from *The Quebec City Crisis*)

Bart Lundrigan

Kelly Block

The camp owner – an athletic-looking man with his blond hair strangely combed over the bald spots – seemed to be dumping on Muck, whom he didn't even know, for being old-fashioned and out of touch with modern coaching techniques. At one point Kelly Block had even said it was "time for the Screech Owls to move on, get a new coach who understands the way the game is played today." Travis had felt his cheeks burn with anger. Already he didn't like Kelly Block.

"Mental Block" was the nickname Nish had already given the head of the sports camp, and it seemed to be sticking – at least when the Owls talked to each other in private.

(from *Danger in Dinosaur Valley*)

Earring

A man was walking towards Travis fast. He had on a dark bulky windbreaker and tinted glasses, the kind that seem to darken as the wearer moves from shadow to light, from inside to outside. He had a buzz-cut, his hair clipped so close his scalp seemed to shine in the arena lights. He had one large earring in his left ear.

(from *The West Coast Murders*)

He wore a long dark overcoat that reached almost to his feet. He had on brand-new Nike sneakers that looked as if they'd never before been tried on, let alone walked in. And he wore a strange, multicoloured hat pulled tight over his ears. Standing there in the shadows of the alley, he was hard to make out, apart from coat, shoes, hat, and beard – almost as if the clothes stood there empty, a clever dummy rigged to look like a very bad character.

(from *Sudden Death in New York City*)

Big

WILLIE GRANGER #8

PLAYER PROFILE

Position
DEFENCE
Height
5'5"
Weight
140 lbs
Shoots
LEFT
Born
REGINA, CANADA
Age
13

Speaking of *The Guinness Book of World Records*, that's my business. I play defence – nothing fancy, get the job done – but I'm also the team trivia expert. I'm the guy with 10,000 hockey cards. I'm also the one with the uncle who writes sports for the *National Post* and gets me all those autographs and neat souvenirs.

You want to know the highest mountain in the Rockies? Ask me. You want to know what the world record is for the longest fingernails or eating dew worms or, for that matter, the tallest person who ever played in the NHL? You ask me.

You want to know who owns the stinkingest hockey bag in the history of the game, you want to know the ugliest nudist in the entire world, you want to know the guy with the dumbest string of yells in the universe? Don't ask me.

Ask number 44, the guy with the beet red face over there in the corner.

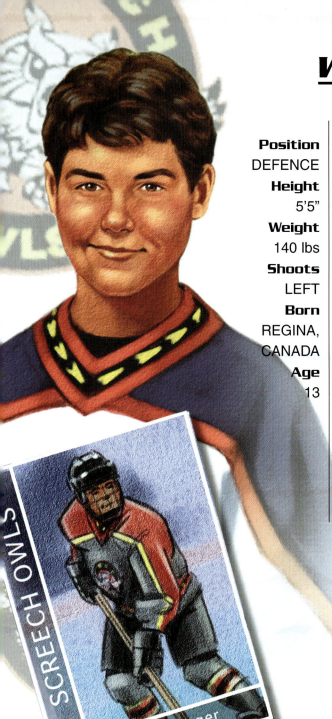

SCOUTING REPORT

POS.	GAMES	GOALS	ASSISTS	POINTS	PIM
D	43	2	7	9	39

"Smart, dependable defencemen who can make the long pass. The type of team player who finds a positive in everything that happens – even one of Nishikawa's bad games!"

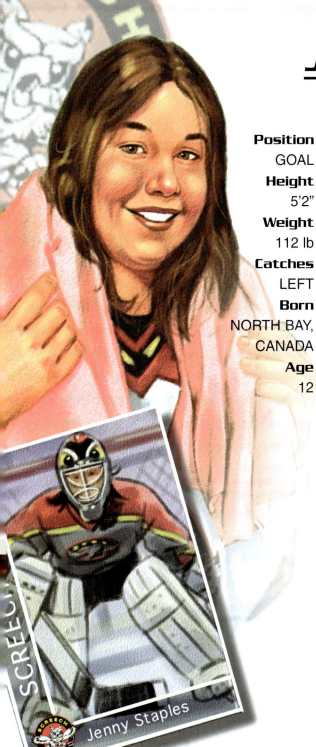

JENNY STAPLES #29

PLAYER PROFILE

Position
GOAL
Height
5'2"
Weight
112 lb
Catches
LEFT
Born
NORTH BAY, CANADA
Age
12

I'm the goaltender on the Screech Owls. Actually, I'm one of two – Jeremy Weathers, my good friend, is the other. We're probably the only two goalies in the world who share a job and don't resent each other.

Muck sometimes jokes that if he could take the best parts of Jeremy and me, he'd be able to put together the best peewee goaltender since Patrick Roy was a little kid. I know what he means. We're so different in everything we do – maybe that's why we get on so well together. I'm good at playing the angles, and Jeremy's a reflex goalie with a lightning-fast glove hand. I play the old stand-up style; he's more a butterfly goalie who goes down fast, stays down, and then twists and turns and kicks his pads high and guesses. His hero is Dominik Hasek, who beat Canada in that shootout in Nagano during the Winter Olympics. My hero is Manon Rhéaume, who doesn't even play any more but who was the first woman goaltender to attract real attention. She even got into an NHL game once. Well, actually it was an exhibition game, but she can always say she played for the Tampa Bay Lightning, which is good enough for me and for probably a couple of hundred other women goaltenders who were first inspired by her.

SCOUTING REPORT

POS.	GAMES	GAA	SV PCT
G	21	3.60	.850

"Staples just keeps getting better and better. Her glove hand is improving and her positioning is excellent. She's also hoping for a future Olympics."

My best friend, though, is Sarah. Sarah and, lately, Sam and Liz. We usually all end up rooming together, so we spend a lot of time together and we've become very close. We all have different interests. I'm into competitive swimming, but sometimes it conflicts with my hockey and I have to take one over the other, which I don't like. But my parents are good about it. They say it's entirely up to me, which sometimes makes the decisions hard to make. One time I'm all swimming, the next all hockey. But hockey is where my best friends are.

Jeremy and I pretty well split the goaltending duties. My only big disappointment was when I couldn't finish that game in Nagano, but when everyone realized I was hurt too badly to go on, the big centre for the other team skated over and tapped my pads in front of everyone. It was so neat of him. It was like the whole team was saluting the way I'd played. My arm was killing me, but the rest of me felt like I'd won the Olympic medal.

The thing about that game was that Jeremy had been unable to come over to Japan with us. I was the only goaltender, and Muck figured I could go all the way, play every game. But when I got hurt we had to put someone else in. Nish, and his ridiculous "force shield."

Don't ask me the rest of the story.

JEREMY WEATHERS #1

PLAYER PROFILE

Position
GOAL

Height
5'3"

Weight
119 lb

Catches
LEFT

Born
TAMARACK, CANADA

Age
12

I'm not very big, which is why I became a goalie. Oddly enough, that's probably why most goaltenders play in the net, which is insane. The coach sees this kid who's too small, or can hardly skate, and he says, "There's our goaltender." Ten years later they're drafting the junior players into the NHL and the announcers are talking about the goaltenders having good size but not been able to skate well enough.

Muck has a better idea. Well before peewee level, everybody should get a chance to play goal. Kids who will never play nets – like Dmitri, for example – can appreciate what we go through when guys like him whip in and roof it. It also makes sure people like me and Jenny learn how to skate properly and also how to handle the puck – otherwise we won't be able to play out. That way, when we do decide that we're full-time goalies and we reach peewee, we can skate and handle the puck an awful lot better than other kids who have been goalies right from Day One.

Goalies are supposed to be crazy. You know all the stories. Patrick Roy talking to his goalposts. Jacques Plante knitting his own underwear. Damian Rhodes booking a hotel room downtown the night before home games so he'd "think" he was playing a road game, because he had better record on the road than at home.

I have no idea if I'll one day be one of those stories. I am a bit nuts, for sure. I like peanut-butter-and-tomato sandwiches. I can only do my homework if the television is on full blast. If I get a shutout I keep the same underwear on until next game and wear it then, too. And I think I'm getting worse.

SCOUTING REPORT

POS.	GAMES	GAA	SV PCT	
G	22	3.59	.849	

"Quick and smart with the puck – Weathers is all reaction, and when he's on his game, the other team is guaranteed to be off theirs. Nice glove hand."

"The Turtle"

"*Pssst!*"

Travis turned just as he was about to dive off the end of the dock. He could barely make Nish out in the shadows.

"*Over here! C'm'ere!*"

Travis hurried in under the diving platform, where Nish was huddled with Andy. Even in the dim light, Travis could see Nish was shivering. And it wasn't a cold evening.

"Y-you two are m-my witnesses, okay?" Nish said.

"Okay," Andy said.

"You're really going to do it?" said Travis.

"Just watch!"

Quick as a flash, Nish dropped his bathing trunks. He dived off the dock, and swam deep under the water, as far out as he could go.

But when he came up, he was screaming.

"TTTTUUUUUURRTTTTLLLE!!!!!!"

Travis couldn't believe his eyes. The water around Nish was foaming as he flailed away. Still screaming, Nish raced for the dock, his arms thrashing desperately in the water.

Halfway back, he stopped, reached down into the water, and shrieked.

"HHHELLLPPPPPP MMMEEEEE!"

Andy and Travis raced to the end of the dock as Nish approached, his flailing arms splashing them both. He reached up, still screaming.

"HE GRABBED ME!! THE TURTLE GRABBED MY TOE!!!"

Others were screaming now and racing to get out. Travis couldn't believe it. Had Mr. Clifford lied to them about snapping turtles? He'd said they'd never attack.

Nish used his friends' outstretched arms to pull himself up and clear of the water.

He reached under the diving platform for his bathing suit. It was gone!

"NNNNNNOOOOOOOOOOO!!!" Nish screamed.

Covering himself with his hands, Nish took off. Stark naked, he ran the length of the dock and onto the shore, past the singsong, which had come to a sudden halt, and up the path to the cabins, screaming all the way.

"NNNNNNNNNNNOOOOOOOOOOOOOOOOOO!!!"

"Go, Naked Boy!"

Sarah was in the water at the end of the dock. She had a scuba mask and snorkel pulled up off her face.

Sarah, the snapping turtle.

(from *Murder at Hockey Camp*)

"Bird Poop"

Nish seemed to be gathering himself. The closer they moved toward the entrance to the Tower of Terror ride, the quieter he became. He stood off to one side of the line, his eyes closed and his arms folded across his chest. He was in another world, dealing with his well-known fear of heights.

Nish didn't even notice when a brilliantly coloured bird landed on a branch directly over him and let go a sloppy white poop that landed directly on top of his head.

"*Scores!*" shouted Lars.

"*Shhhhhh!*" hissed Sarah, jumping directly in front of Nish and turning to the rest of the Owls, most of whom were pointing and laughing at him standing there with his eyes closed.

"*Don't anybody tell him!*" whispered Sarah. "Not a word. Promise?"

The Owls all stifled their giggles.

Incredibly, no one said anything as the line continued to inch forward. Nish seemed only half awake, moving with the flow. A few tourists noticed, but each time they were stopped from saying anything by the Owls.

Soon, all eyes were on the entrance to the ride, all ears on the grinding gears and sliding cables and terrifying, hideous screams that came from above. Travis quickly checked the last sentence on the warning sign:

"*Visitors who wish to change their minds may exit to the right.*"

For a moment he was undecided. He looked up toward the "service elevator," where the next trip was being loaded. Some were already screaming. A young woman lunged back towards the doorway, already in tears, but her boyfriend grabbed her and hauled her forward. Those waiting for the next ride laughed.

Travis couldn't take it. When he was sure no one was looking, he bolted for the safety exit. Through a doorway and up a quick, open elevator, and he was out into the Florida sunshine and could breathe again.

He had chickened out.

Travis was miserable. Even if he covered his ears, he could still hear the sounds of the Tower of Terror – the cables slipping, the gears grinding, the trapdoors breaking open, the rush of wind as the elevator plummeted again and again, and the endless, chilling screaming.

He waited around for the others by the exit, where he found a handy washroom. There was also a souvenir store, where they sold everything from T-shirts that bragged "I survived the Tower of Terror" to coffee mugs depicting the attraction. The store even had a booth where they sold photos that must have been taken at the very top of the tower, when the riders were at their most terrified. Their hair was standing on end!

Travis watched as laughing, relieved riders came off the ride and entered the shop. Feeling like a fool, like a traitor to his own team, he ducked behind a rack of souvenir coffee cups.

He heard the Owls coming even before he saw them. Loudest, of course, was Nish, and he was in full brag.

"*It was nothin', man!*"

They all rounded the corner at once, a laughing, pushing, shoving throng of kids in T-shirts they'd picked up everywhere from Lake Placid, New York, to Malmö, Sweden. A few had Screech Owls caps on. Nish, of course, had another type of cap on. The bird poop was still there. It had survived the trip!

"Hey!" Nish shouted. "Let's check out the pictures!"

Travis could see Data wink at Lars. The Owls hurried to see the expression on Nish's face when he saw what was lying on top of his hair. Travis slipped unnoticed into the group.

"Great ride, eh, Trav?" Andy said as Travis edged up beside him.

"Yeah " Travis said. "Great."

"Which one were you on? I didn't see you."

"The other elevator."

Travis winced a bit. Technically, he wasn't lying. It obviously had been a great ride, and he had taken the other elevator. But not the next elevator on the ride.

"WHAT THE –!?" Nish shouted.

The man running the photo booth had just put up the photograph of the Owls' ride. Sarah's long hair was standing straight up, as was Lars's. Nish's hair was sitting flat, most of it trapped under a white mess.

"This picture didn't come out right!" Nish practically shouted at the man.

The man merely looked at the top of Nish's head and shrugged, smiling slightly.

"Looks pretty accurate to me," he said.

Nish slipped one hand up to his ear, then carefully onto his hair and up to the top of his head, where he found what he feared.

"Who did this?" he demanded, turning on the other Owls.

Willie, the trivia expert, answered: "I believe it was a cardinal."

(from *Terror in Florida*)

"Gauchies on the Flag Pole"

"WHERE ARE MY GAUCHIES?"

The players had just come back from an early morning dip in the Ottawa River and were supposed to change quickly for the long bus ride to Algonquin Park. Nish had been first in the water, first out of the water, first dried off, and first back to the tent. Travis was only stepping off the beach when he heard the yells from inside their tent.

"WHO TOOK MY GAUCHIES?"

Travis hurried up, pulled back the flaps, and there was Nish, buck naked in the centre of the tent, kicking everyone's sleeping bags and clothes as fast as his feet could move. He seemed near panic.

"*My boxers are gone!*" he shouted at Travis, as if Travis would know what had become of them. "All of them. What the hell's going on here?"

"Calm down," Travis said. "You've just misplaced them like you do with everything."

"Somebody's stolen them."

"Who'd want to touch your boxer shorts?" Fahd asked as he ducked inside.

"That's what I want to know," cried Nish, missing Fahd's point.

Travis, who was the most organized, led them on a careful check of all their clothes. This wasn't the first time they'd been on a hunt like this: Travis still chuckled when he remembered how Nish's boxers had once ended up in the freezer. The boys carefully made piles of Lars's stuff, and Fahd's, and Andy's, Jesse's, Dmitri's, Travis's, Nish's – but nowhere could they find any of Nish's distinctive yellow-and-green boxer shorts.

"Call the police," Nish said.

"And what?" Travis asked. "Ask them to put out an all-points-bulletin on missing underwear? You'll just have to borrow some."

"Not mine!" said Fahd with alarm.

"Not mine!"

"Not mine, either!"

"Nor mine!"

"Forget it," Nish said angrily. "They're all too small anyway."

They poked around in the clothes some more, but it was futile. Finally Nish sighed heavily, a sign that he was giving up.

"What'll you do?" asked Fahd.

"Go naked, pal – that okay with you? Will you mind my big white butt sitting on your lap?"

105

"Oh, God!" said Fahd. "Can't you find something?"

"You can wear your bathing suit," Travis suggested. "We'll probably be swimming again anyway."

"It's wet."

"So what? Put it on."

Nish made a face and stepped back into his bathing suit, then pulled his wide khaki shorts over top. The wet bathing suit immediately soaked through to the front of his shorts.

"Jeez," said Nish. "Now I look like I wet myself!"

"Better that than naked," said Fahd. "C'mon! Let's go – we're already five minutes late."

They finished dressing, grabbed their towels, and ran to catch the team bus, which Mr. Dillinger had already pulled up to the front gate of the camp. The rest of the Owls were already aboard, and a great cheer went up when the stragglers came into sight.

Nish, worried about the wet spots on his shorts, wrapped his swimming towel around himself as he ran. He was last to the bus, and had to wait while the others filed by Mr. Dillinger.

Joe Hall was already there. He shook a finger at each late boy, but didn't really seem all that angry. His eyes went wide when he saw Nish wrapped in a damp towel.

"You got anything on under there, big boy?" shouted Sam from well back in the bus.

Nish looked up, his face reddening. "Somebody stole my boxers. You wouldn't know anything about that, would you?"

The whole bus broke into laughter. They'd been waiting for this moment.

"Check the flagpole!" Jenny shouted.

Nish looked from face to face, but saw no allies, no explanation. Finally, he bent down and leaned towards the window, staring up as far as he could see.

There, at the top of the camp flagpole, Nish's boxer shorts flapped in a gentle breeze.

"Who did that?" Nish asked, unnecessarily.

"*We did!*" the girls on the team all said at once.

(from *The Ghost of the Stanley Cup*)

MR. DILLINGER – TEAM MANAGER

MANAGER PROFILE

Sometimes I wonder what I've unleashed here. It seems the only thing people ever ask me about is the Stupid Stop.

The Screech Owls all tell the other kids they get to know on other teams, and the next thing you know I'll have some team manager on the phone begging me to let him in on the Screech Owls' "secret weapon." A couple of times I've even had our own parents call me up and demand that I explain.

What right do I have, they want to know, to destroy every good value they've ever tried to pass on to their beloved little baby?

Good heavens, I feel like telling them. Lighten up! Smell the coffee! Take a time out! Get a life!

Here's what the Stupid Stop is – to me, at least. I've got a busload of kids with more pressure on their young lives that they need. They've got pressure on them to win, even if they play for, in my opinion, the best darn and most sensible peewee hockey coach in the world. They've got pressure on them to excel, whether it's in school or in sports – and a lot of them play more than just hockey. They put pressure on each other, which is the way a good team should work. That's healthy pressure, because they believe, as Muck tells them, that they win as a team and they lose as a team. But it's still pressure, pressure, pressure. Every day of their lives. Pressure, pressure, pressure.

So, what's the Stupid Stop? It's anti-pressure. It's the opposite of pressure. It's total non-pressure. And I believe every kid has a right to feel at least as much non-pressure as real pressure. Childhood is a short, precious time – and where do we adults get the right to spoil it for them?

Anyway, I came up with the Stupid Stop completely by accident and now it's probably the finest

MR. DILLINGER – TEAM MANAGER

tradition of the Screech Owls Hockey Club. All I did one day on a long road trip – I think we were headed to Montreal – was pull over at this little roadside stop that had a couple of gas pumps and one of the those old-fashioned country general stores and, while I was gassing up the bus, I gave each one of them two bucks with strict instructions to buy something absolutely useless.

What'd it cost me? Thirty bucks? So what. You never saw kids have so much fun in your life, I swear. Best bargain I ever bought.

Here's why I think it works. These kids have grown up with parents who have very high expectations. They want their little darling to do well in school and do well in sports because that way they'll do well in life. But it's all about pressure, the way I see it. Someone, maybe a grandparent, or an uncle, gives them a few dollars for their birthday or Christmas or something, and what's the first thing they hear? "Now you put that away for your education." "Now don't you spend that all in one place."

All I do is reverse that and see what happens. I tell them that here's their money – usually a couple of bucks, but I've gone as high as five to test them – and they only get it if they undertake to: one, spend it all, immediately; two, spend it all in one place, and; three, use it to buy something that's of absolutely of no use in the world to anyone and won't last more than a couple of days at most.

It drives them crazy! They don't know what to do with it – buy junk food, buy a *Cracked* magazine, buy a stupid pair of fake X-ray glasses like that maniac Nishikawa (love him! love him!), drop it all in those ridiculous machines where you try and pick up a watch with a crane but end up with nothing. It doesn't matter what they do with it, just that they do *something* with it – and it drives them into a frenzy.

I'd love to see some open-minded educator have a serious look at the Stupid Stop. My bet is that it's every bit as educational as Careers Day at school. But then, they'd probably just turn it into another pressure on the poor kids – which would kind of defeat my purpose, wouldn't it?

Anyway, I do other stuff as well. I drive the bus. It's a terrible old bus, a "retired" school bus I picked up for so little I'd be embarrassed to have anyone know. But it makes sense. Rather than have a half-dozen parents and their cars come along on every trip, I get the parents to chip in on

costs and we easily cover the gas and insurance on the old tub. Muck says he likes it because it encourages the parents to stay at home – but I'd never tell any of them that!

I drive the bus and take care of the equipment and do the skate sharpening. If we're camping, which we sometimes do, I'm in charge of breakfast. I do this thing the kids call "The Mr. D. Special" – pancakes, sausages, hash brown potatoes, toast, and, on top of the pancakes, a scoop of blueberry ice cream. The kids claim they play a lot better after one of them. Muck isn't so sure.

I tried coaching, but I'm just one of those guys who's absolutely no good at sports – makes you wonder if Derek's really my boy, doesn't it? – and so I found other things to do. I'm well-organized. I make sure we have everything from fresh rolls of shinpad tape to the latest CDs for the ride. I have my first aid, which has come in handy more times than I'd care to admit. Nishikawa (love that nutbar!) probably wouldn't be playing the game if it hadn't been for that first-aid course I took and me making him lie perfectly still until the ambulance came that time he took a header into the boards. I do pretty well everything I can for the Owls.

I guess that makes me an enthusiast. I've been known to get a bit too enthusiastic – I made a proper fool of myself down at Lake Placid – but I'm learning. I'm a great believer that maturity is a life-long process, not a card they give you when you turn eighteen, and I've still got a ways to go. I may have a bald spot and a big pot belly, but maybe that belly just means I've got a great big kid still inside me.

Sometimes I think Derek is more mature than I am. But sometimes I think he's a little too serious for his age and just needs something to remind him what being a kid's all about.

Like another Stupid Stop!

MR. DILLINGER – TEAM MANAGER

MUCK MUNRO – COACH

COACH PROFILE

I have no time for phonies.

I don't like coaches who insist on being called "Coach." I don't like flashy track pants and fancy matching jackets with the guy's name and "Coach" or "Instructor" stitched over the heart. I wouldn't be caught dead in a suit coaching a kids' peewee hockey game and chomping on ice like I'm about to be interviewed between periods on *Hockey Night in Canada*. I don't have any time for coaches who yell at their kids – and even less time for coaches who yell at the youngsters who are out there trying to learn how to referee. I don't like shouters. I don't like bullies. And I don't like coaches who run up the score. Never humiliate an opponent.

What I do like is kids. Actually, that kind of came as a surprise to me. I don't have any of my own. I'm not married – I was once, but that was a long, long time ago, and let's just say it didn't work out and not waste everybody's time here. I'm not married, no kids, and now I find myself spending half my life working with a bunch of crazy twelve- and thirteen-year-olds and the other half of it worrying about them.

It's crazy how I even got into this thing. I was perfectly happy. I had a good job working for the telephone company, putting lines into cottages and the like, and I was doing a lot of fishing in summer and playing a little pickup hockey with the guys in winter. An oldtimers' league where they are so slow you could time them with a sun dial, and where the most important player on the ice is the guy who's responsibility it was to bring the beer that week. You get the picture. Nothing serious.

I'd once been very serious about the game. I grew up in Tamarack, played some lacrosse and ball and a lot of hockey. I wasn't the most talented, but I worked harder than anyone. I'd take on anyone and I'd hit anyone, didn't matter how big or good he was. I was a fair puck-handler, had a pretty good shot, and if I wasn't a fancy skater I was at least quick enough to keep up. Every year I made the all-star team, and then, when I was fifteen, I got asked to come to the camp of the Hamilton Red Wings. This was in the old days, remember, when teams had "territorial rights" over players as young as fourteen, if you can believe it. The Detroit Red Wings owned Hamilton, and Hamilton "owned" Tamarack and dozens of other little towns. I was Red Wings property from the time I was fourteen. If they had the same system today, Canada would probably be thrown out of the United Nations for child slavery. But that's the way it was.

I had a pretty good camp and a fair rookie year. I was a bit behind Paul Henderson, who was our best player, and Paul was different from the other players. He never acted like he was better than anyone else. I learned a lot from him, and we became great friends. He went on to the NHL with the Red Wings and I guess I figured I'd soon follow – except in my second year I broke my leg.

That doesn't sound the same today as it did back then. Today a player breaks something, or even blows a knee, and everyone expects he'll be off a while and then come back good as ever. I had three operations on my leg. First time to set pins in, and second time to break it all over again and set more pins in, and third time I think just so the doctors could see what a mess they'd made of it. My leg was never the same. It's still shorter than the other and doesn't bend too well. I can skate, but barely, and it's sore for days if I'm stupid enough to play a game of scrimmage with the kids – which I do too often. But what can you do? I love the game and I can't dream my leg back and, besides, it's too late anyway. I learned a long, long time ago there's no use crying over spilt beer.

Don Dillinger got me back into the game. He was trying to organize a peewee team in town. He had some pretty good talent, but, to put it kindly, he didn't have a clue what he was doing. Don't get me wrong. Hockey, all sports, need their Don Dillingers – good-hearted volunteers who will do everything under the sun for the kids. But they're better left to organize and manage than coach. To give him credit, he knew it, and that's why he came to me.

"Why should I?" I asked him.

"Because you live here," he said.

"What's that got to do with it?"

"Do you like Tamarack?"

"Never lived anywhere else. I guess I must."

"Did you play hockey here?"

"You know the answer to that – of course I did."

"And did you flood your own ice and sharpen your own skates and teach yourself how to play and find sweaters and socks and equipment for exactly the right number of kids so you could have a team and have some fun?"

"Of course not," I said. "What're you getting at?"

"Just that somebody has to do these things – why not you?"

I couldn't really argue with that. Okay, I told Don, I'll give it a try, but if I don't like it after a week, I'm out of here.

That was more years ago than I can remember. I've been a peewee coach longer than some of the guys I played with lasted in the NHL.

This team, though, the Screech Owls, they are the best I ever had. Sarah Cuthbertson is about the smoothest skater I've seen since Paul Henderson. We got three fine lines, some good backups, sharp goaltending, and, with Sarah, Travis, and Dmitri, probably the most explosive first line in the loop.

We also have Nishikawa. I sometimes think it's fortunate I didn't start out with him. I never would have lasted that first week. But by the time he reached peewee, I'd been there so long I figured I'd seen everything under the sun.

How wrong I was.

It took me a long time to figure out Nishikawa. I tried pushing him, praising him, telling him what an idiot he was, trying to explain on the chalkboard what he should have done – even tried throwing up my arms in despair.

It took me months to find the right buttons to push. I hardly say a word to him. If he acts up, he's benched. Simple as that. I noticed one day that the more important the game gets, the more he decides to play the game. He knows I'll bench him if he's acting silly out there. He also knows that if the game is in doubt, I'll rely on him. How much ice times he gets is completely up to him. It's sort of like we have an agreement.

But I have to admit, when he decides the game matters, he's a heck of a hockey player. I figure if I don't see him in the NHL one day, he might be on the comedy channel – or perhaps on *America's Most Wanted*.

There's not much else to say about me. I'm no fan of expensive new equipment. I tell the kids they might as well dip their hands in wet cement as get a new pair of hockey gloves every year. Gloves are no good until they're fully broken in. And I can't stand parents who scream at their kids from the stands. I love history, everything from the early explorers in Canada to the great battlefields of the American Civil War. I love outdoor shinny and I despise sports bars.

I don't even watch hockey on television when I'm home. I can't bear the way those announcers use their silly telestrators to describe things that are just not true. They act like hockey is some kind of "football" game on ice, with set plays and everything planned out, and they draw all these lines and circles to show what should have happened or what shouldn't have happened. They don't realize that in hockey things just happen. Everyone has the basic skills, everyone knows the basic rules about where you should be and what your responsibilities are – and after that it's pure chaos. What these announcers fail to comprehend is that's the beauty of the game. That's where a Gretzky is able to make something out of nothing. That's where the magic is – not in some diagram that's supposed to explain what just happened out there.

Another thing about television is they only show you the puck. A camera chasing a puck is as useless as a player chasing the puck. For me, the game *away* from the puck is often more interesting, which is why if I can't watch a game live, I don't bother.

But then, I know I'm different. And I'm proud of it.

I once wrote down, mostly for my own interest, my Ten Most Important Rules of Coaching. For what they're worth, I pass them on to all the coaches out there who are trying to do the right thing.

1. Never take yourself, or your game, too seriously. If a sport isn't fun, it's no longer sport.
2. Treat everyone with dignity, no matter what their ability – or, for that matter, their age.
3. Yelling draws attention to you when you are at your worst. The quieter you speak to a person, the louder they hear you.
4. Parents require as much coaching as children. Never let the game be taken away by those who are old enough to know better.
5. Kids should look forward to practice as much as to games. Practice should mean more ice time, more fun, and more improvement. Good practice makes for good games.
6. A pat on the back has never been known to injure a player.
7. We learn from our mistakes, and if you make players afraid to make mistakes, they will stop trying to learn.

MUCK MUNRO – COACH

8. No one is more important than the team. No one is less important than the team.
9. No one – coaches, players, or parents – should look upon this as a career. Games are not jobs.
10. If you can't laugh at yourself, rest assured others are laughing at you.
11. **(Bonus)** No coach should have to put up with more than one Nishikawa per lifetime.

Nish's Greatest Madcap Schemes

"The Mosquito and Shaving Cream Trick"

Nish and Andy tiptoed over to the bunk where Data lay mumbling in deep sleep. . . . Very carefully, Nish began to fill Data's right hand with shaving cream from an aerosol can. When he had built up a nice big mound, he capped the can and slipped it back under the bunk.

Nish gave Andy the thumbs-up. Andy pushed the play button on the boom box and the buzz of the mosquito began. Andy turned up the volume and moved the tape recorder even closer. Data stirred, mumbling.

The taped "mosquito" landed. Andy pulled the boom box away. Nish leaned over and poked the feather just under Data's nose, then ran it down over his mouth and onto his chin.

Slap!

Data's right hand came up and smacked into the imaginary mosquito, sending shaving cream spattering into his face and pillow. Data mumbled, but didn't wake up.

"*Perfect!*" hissed Nish, backing away from the bunk.

"Better than we thought" whispered Andy.

"Why Data?" Travis asked.

"Test case," said Nish. "Nothing personal."

"What do you mean, 'test case'?"

"If it worked this well on Data" grinned Nish, "think how great it'll look on our good friend, Buddy O'Reilly."

(from Murder at Hockey Camp)

"The Goalie Force Shield"

"Great goaltenders," Nish announced, "are nuttier than fruitcakes. You have to be eccentric to play goal."

He went down the list of great goalies as if counting off points for an exam. Jacques Plante, who used to knit his own underwear. Glenn Hall, who used to throw up before every game and between periods. Patrick Roy, who talked to goal posts and insisted on stepping over the lines in the ice rather than skating over them. Goalies who had secret messages painted on their masks. Goalies who talked to themselves throughout the game, as if they were not only playing but also doing the play-by-play.

"Mr. Imoo's going to help me," Nish announced as they walked along.

"He's going to work with me until I'm the first goalie in history to have a force shield."

"A *what?*" Travis asked.

"He's an expert in martial arts, too – not just a Buddhist priest. He's the greatest guy I ever met. He's got a black belt in judo and he knows tae kwon do, and he's going to teach me how to do the Indonesian 'force shield.' It's a little-known Asian secret that'll give me superhuman powers."

"You already have superhuman power," said Sarah. "Unfortunately, it's in your butt."

(from *Nightmare in Nagano*)

"Blowing Up the Outhouse"

"I've figured it out," Nish said.

Travis didn't dare ask what. How to behave during a hockey game? How to be a real team player? It could have been anything.

They were lying in the tent, a light rain drumming on the canvas. They'd practised earlier and had eaten and were resting.

"Figured what out?" Fahd finally asked. He couldn't resist.

"How I'm going to get her."

"Get who?"

"Oh, just the one who tried to make a fool of me on the river, just the one who put my gauchies up the flagpole, just the biggest pain in the butt this team has ever known, that's all."

Travis couldn't resist. "Who's that?" he asked.

"Very funny," said Nish. He was sucking loudly on a Tootsie Roll, offering none around as usual, and thinking out loud, also as usual. "It's got to be embarrassing, right? Really embarrassing."

"Why?" Fahd asked.

"Because she embarrassed me. All that '*Kawa-bun-ga*' crap and stealing my boxers. It's got to be just as good from my side."

"Let it go," said Travis. "She's a good sport. The team likes her."

"This isn't about the team," countered Nish. "This is about her and me."

"You're too competitive," said Lars.

"Not at all," said Nish. "I'm just getting even. Like in a tie game. What's competitive about that? I don't have to win, just get even."

Yeah, right, Travis thought to himself. *Who's he kidding?* But he said nothing.

Nish went on. "You know where the women's washroom is?"

"You mean the outhouse," Fahd corrected.

"Whatever – you know where I mean."

"You'd better be careful there," warned Travis.

"Nah. She has to go sometime, doesn't she? I mean, girls do go to the bathroom, don't they?"

Lars couldn't believe it. "You want us to sing, 'We-know-where-you're-go-ing'? That's a bit childish even for you, isn't it?"

"Nah, no singing. I got a much more sophisticated plan than that. Say she goes in and shuts the door, and a few seconds later there's this enormous explosion that everybody in the camp hears. You think she wouldn't find that a bit embarrassing?"

"You can't bomb an outhouse!" protested Fahd.

"Not a bomb, stupid – a harmless cannon cracker. Like the ones they set off on Canada Day."

"Where are you going to get a cannon cracker?"

"They sell fireworks at that little shop," he said.

"Not to kids they don't," said Travis.

"They'll sell to me," said Nish. "Just you watch."

(from *The Ghost of the Stanley Cup*)

"Elvis Nishikawa"

After he had his shin pads and pants on, Travis went out and walked up and down the corridor in his socks. All along the walls were huge, photographs of famous people who had played Madison Square Garden. He walked along, checking the names: Elton John, Frank Sinatra, Judy Garland, the Beatles, Wayne Nishikawa . . .

Wayne Nishikawa?

Travis stopped so abruptly he slipped in his socks and almost fell.

Nish?

Taped over the photograph, with black hockey tape, was one of Nish's hockey cards from the Quebec Peewee tournament. Nish's smiling mug was covering the face of Elvis Presley. Nish's name – cut, it seemed, from the program for the Big Apple tournament – had also been taped over Elvis Presley's name at the bottom of the framed picture. Nish's mother would have been outraged. She called Elvis Presley "The King" and had most of his records.

"Like it?" a voice called from down the corridor.

It was Nish, half-dressed, sticking his head out the dressing-room door. He was grinning.

"I'm sure Elvis would be pleased," said Travis.

"He's dead," Nish said. "I'm the new King."

"King of what?" Travis asked.

"King of Hockey," Nish began. "King a da Big Apple. King of the *Guinness Book of World Records* – you name it."

Okay, Travis thought, I will. He forced a grin back at his weird friend: "King of Jerks."

Nish suddenly looked hurt. "What's dat for?" he asked.

"You're acting stupid," Travis said. "You're going way overboard on everything. That stupid New York talk. That stupid mooning idea that's just going to get everybody in trouble."

"Relax," Nish said, his old grin rising back into his face. "Nobody's gonna get hurt."

"They better not," said Travis.

Nish shook his head. "Relax, pal. Enjoy the Big Apple. And don't forget – one day you'll be able to say you knew me."

"What good's that, even if you do it? It's not like anybody's going to know it's you."

"My butt will be world-famous," Nish said. "It'll be like saying you saw Niagara Falls being formed, or the pyramids being built – you know what I mean?"

Travis just shook his head. No, he didn't know what Nish meant. And when he tried to force his mind to work it through, it was like his brain was a computer that had suddenly crashed.

(from *Sudden Death in New York City*)

"The Pop Trick"

When the movie slowed for some dull romantic development, Nish scooted out of his seat and made for the refreshment counter. He came back with two tall drinks and handed one to Travis, who took it and sighed deep into his seat. Perhaps the drink would shut Nish up; at least he wouldn't be able to shout with his mouth wrapped around a straw.

But Nish had no intention of drinking his huge pop. He pulled out the straw and dropped it on the floor. He twisted off the plastic lid and dropped that, too. Then, to Travis's astonishment, Nish began spilling out his drink. Travis cringed, hearing the liquid splash onto the floor.

The theatre floor, made of polished concrete, slanted downward towards the screen, so the liquid immediately ran away under the rows of seats in front.

Is he nuts? Travis wondered.

Nish began splashing in the liquid with his feet, picking up his sneakers and slapping them down hard. It sounded like he was running through a deep puddle. "*Gross!*" he called out.

A couple sitting up ahead turned and stared. Nish splashed again, faking that he was disgusted. He turned around and angrily faced an innocent-looking young man sitting alone about three seats directly behind.

"What's the matter?" Nish called. "Can't you use the bathroom?"

The man blinked, not comprehending. Up ahead, the young couple began scrambling. The pop had washed up as far as their feet now, and they made squishy sounds as they left their seats and hurried for the safety of the aisle. The young man reached for his girlfriend's hand and pulled her. She slipped and went down, screaming. Her boyfriend raised his fist at the startled man sitting behind Nish.

"*You pig!*" he screamed. "*Use the washroom!*"

Travis sank even lower in his seat. He could feel the body beside him shaking: Nish, in full giggle. The young man up front, after helping his girlfriend to her feet, charged up the aisle.

Not knowing what was going on, but sure something bad was about to happen, the man behind Nish scurried out of his seat as the boyfriend came at him. There was the sound of clothes ripping.

"Fight!" Nish shouted. "FIGHT! FIGHT!"

The theatre erupted in whistles and shouts. The movie ground to a halt, the lights came on, and Mr. Dinsmore and several attendants hurried down the aisle closest to Travis and Nish. It took only a few moments to break up the fight. It took slightly longer, with the lights full on, to find out that the whole thing was a misunderstanding, that the disgusting liquid was nothing more than Sprite.

Nish's Sprite.

"*Get out!*" Mr. Dinsmore shouted at Travis and Nish. "*Get out of my theatre, both of you!*"

(from *Horror on River Road*)

"The World Record for Mooning"

"Times Square is going to be the big thing at New Year's," said Jenny Staples, the backup goaltender. "There might be a million people there."

"And more than a billion watching on TV," added Fahd.

"They'll have the countdown on that big screen," said Derek. "I think it might be the biggest in the world."

Nish came suddenly alert. He sat up sharply, his face flushing with excitement. "How many?" he asked Fahd.

"A billion, I think."

"It's televised?"

"All over the world. You've seen it. Everybody's seen the countdown."

"*Live?*" Nish asked, his face gleaming.

"Of course live, you idiot," shouted Sam, looking up from retying her skates. "It's the countdown for the New Year. You think they tape it and play it the next day?"

Everyone laughed, but not Nish.

"Live? One billion people watching?"

"Yeah," said Sarah. "So?"

"So," Nish said triumphantly, turning on Fahd. "Is there anything in the *Guinness Book of World Records* on 'mooning'?"

Fahd looked up, incredulous. "What?"

"*Mooning* – what's the world's record for mooning? If I mooned a billion people at once, would I get in?"

Travis looked across the room at Sarah, who rolled her eyes and sighed. Travis tried to cut off his imagination, but it had already raced ahead of him. He could see the crowd at Times Square. He could see the big video monitor and hear the countdown: Ten! . . . Nine! . . . Eight! . . . Seven! . . . Six! . . . Five! . . . Four! . . . Three! . . . Two! . . . One!

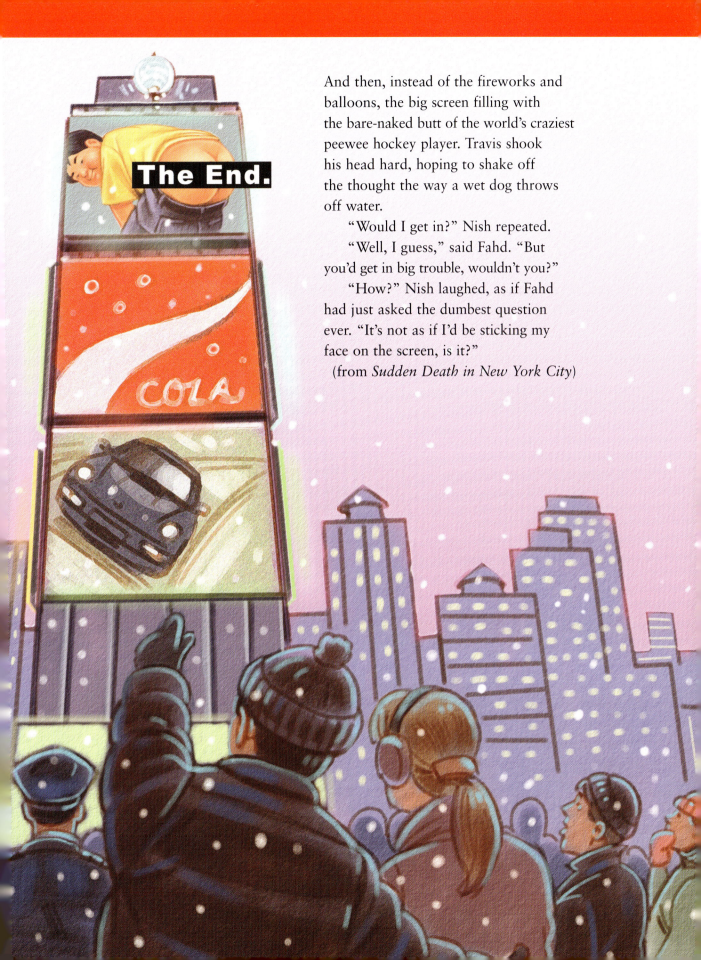

The End.

And then, instead of the fireworks and balloons, the big screen filling with the bare-naked butt of the world's craziest peewee hockey player. Travis shook his head hard, hoping to shake off the thought the way a wet dog throws off water.

"Would I get in?" Nish repeated.

"Well, I guess," said Fahd. "But you'd get in big trouble, wouldn't you?"

"How?" Nish laughed, as if Fahd had just asked the dumbest question ever. "It's not as if I'd be sticking my face on the screen, is it?"

(from *Sudden Death in New York City*)

ROSTER CHANGES

The Night They Stole the Stanley Cup
Sarah Cuthbertson moved onto Aeros.
Matt Brown moved away.
Zak Adelman and Mario Terziano off team.
Goalies Guy Boucher (off to AA-level hockey) and Sareen Goupa (to women's team) gone from team.
New goalies Jeremy Weathers and Jenny Staples.
Derek Dillinger moved to first line to take Sarah's spot.
Andy Higgins new centre on team.

Liz Moscovitz, left wing, new to team, friend of Sarah's. Chantal Larochelle, new winger, from Montreal. Lars Johanssen, from Sweden, joins team.

Murder at Hockey Camp
Sarah comes back to team for summer camp.

Kidnapped in Sweden
Sarah travels with team to Sweden to experience big European ice surface.

Terror in Florida
Simon Milliken joins team.
Sarah back on team – *permanently*.

The Ghost of the Stanley Cup
Samantha Bennett joins the team on defence.
Replaces Larry Ulmar – Data – whose spine has been injured.

RECORD OF ALL GAMES PLAYED

Lake Placid Peewee International Championship
1. Owls versus Portland Panthers
   Score: 3-3 tie
   Goals: Dmitri, Matt, Derek
   Goaltender: Guy
   Turning Point: With two minutes to go in the game, Travis beats two Panthers and slips a perfect pass to Derek, who fires a quick shot to the open short side.
2. Owls versus Duluth Dodgers
   Score: 4-0 Owls
   Goals: Derek (2), Matt, Dmitri
   Goaltender: Guy
   Turning Point: Sarah sets up early rush, passes to Dmitri, who drops back to Nish who hits Derek coming in on the far side. Derek has whole empty net to shoot at.
3. Owls versus Toronto Towers
   Score: 4-2 Owls
   Goals: Derek, Dmitri, Matt, Travis (empty net)
   Goaltender: Sareen
   Turning point: After Owls fall behind, Dmitri ties game on clear breakaway.
4. Owls versus Portland Panthers (Championship Game)
   Score: 3-2 Owls
   Goals: Dmitri, Derek (2)
   Goaltender: Guy
   Turning Point: Travis sets up Derek for winning goal.
   Key Opponents: Billings and Yantha play brilliantly in losing cause.
   SCREECH OWLS WIN CHAMPIONSHIP!

The Little Stanley Cup, Toronto
1. Owls versus Albany River Rats
   Score: 7-1 Owls
   Goals: Dmitri (2), Gordie, Lars, Andy, Jesse, Chantal
   Goaltender: Jenny
   Turning Point: Data sends Dmitri in on clean breakaway, Dmitri scores on a high, hard slapper.
2. Owls versus Montreal Vedettes
   Score: 2-1 Vedettes
   Goals: Dmitri
   Goaltender: Jeremy
   Turning Point: Travis fails to score on break in final minutes, putting high backhand off crossbar.
3. Owls versus Muskoka Wildlife
   Score: 3-2 Owls
   Goals: Dmitri, Liz, Lars
   Goaltender: Jenny
   Turning Point: Owls fight back from being down 2-0, Travis fakes shot and feeds Lars for pretty goal that puts Owls ahead 3-2.

4. Owls versus Toronto Towers (Championship Game)
   Score: 5-4 Towers
   Goals: Dmitri (2), Andy, Lars
   Goaltender: Jenny
   Turning Point: Towers score off a scramble in dying seconds to put game into overtime, Towers scored on first shot in overtime.

First Nations Peewee Hockey Tournament, Waskaganish
1. Owls versus Moose Factory Mighty Geese
   Score: 5-2 Owls
   Goals: Dmitri (2), Travis, Liz, Andy
   Goaltender: Jenny
   Turning Point: Dmitri catches Mighty Geese on bad line change and flies in, untouched, on net to score.
2. Owls versus Great Whale Belugas
   Score: 4-1 Owls
   Goals: Derek, Andy, Chantal, Lars
   Goaltender: Jeremy
   Turning Point: Dmitri drops puck to Travis, Travis dekes goaltender and slips puck over to Derek for open net goal.
3. Owls versus Waskaganish Wolverines (Championship Game)
   Score: 2-1 Wolverines
   Goals: Jesse
   Goaltender: Chantal
   Turning Point: Rachel Highboy, Jesse's cousin, sets up Jimmy Whiskeyjack for Wolverines' winning goal.

Summer Hockey Camp World Peewee Championship, Huntsville
Owls versus Toronto Junior Aeros
Score: 4-4
Goals: Dmitri, Gordie, Nish, Travis. (Sarah scores three goals for Aeros)
Goaltender: Jeremy
Turning Point: Sarah fools Nish on rush and scores tying goal in fun exhibition game.

International Goodwill Peewee Tournament, Sweden
1. Owls versus CSKA (Slava Shadrin's Moscow team)
   Score: 6-3 CSKA
   Goals: Dmitri, Sarah, Andy
   Goaltending: Jenny
   Turning Point: Slava splits Owls' defence, dekes around Jenny, spins and scores goal by dropping puck between his own legs – eight seconds into the game.
2. Owls versus Tampere, Finland.
   Score: 3-1 Owls
   Goals: Andy, Sarah, Lars

   Goaltender: Jeremy
   Turning Point: Sarah and Dmitri get a two-on-one break, Sarah fakes pass to Dmitri and slides hard backhander in off far post.
3. Owls versus Gothenburg
   Score: 3-2 Owls
   Goals: Dmitri (2), Nish
   Goaltender: Jenny
   Note: Travis and Sarah did not play, recovering from injuries after kidnapping.
   Turning point: Nish scores winning goal on hard drive from the point.
4. Owls versus CSKA (Championship Game)
   Score: 4-3 Owls (Owls win shootout)
   Goals: Travis (2), Dmitri
   Goaltender: Jeremy
   Turning Point: Travis scores goal with 34 seconds left – same time as Paul Henderson scored winning goal in 1972 – but Slava ties up in dying moments. Game goes to overtime shootout: Lars and Nish score in shootout to give Canada the win.
   OWLS WIN CHAMPIONSHIP!

Spring Break Tournament, Orlando and Lakeland, Florida
1. Owls versus Ann Arbor Wings
   Score: 4-2 Owls
   Goals: Dmitri, Andy, Derek, Simon
   Goaltender: Jeremy
   Turning Point: Simon sweeps around defence and pops backhander over goalie's shoulder to give Owls 4-1 lead.
2. Owls versus Boston Mini-Bruins
   Score: 3-2 Owls
   Goals: Nish, Sarah, Travis
   Goaltender: Jenny
   Turning Point: Nish play at blueline, sets up Travis.
3. Owls versus State Selects
   Score: 3-2 Owls
   Goals: Simon, Dmitri, Nish
   Goaltender: Jenny
   Turning Point: After being down 2-0, Owls stag remarkable comeback, winning game on Nish's unbelievable Mario Lemieux' between-the-legs shot.
   OWLS WIN CHAMPIONSHIP!

Quebec International Peewee Tournament, Quebec City
1. Owls versus Halifax Hurricanes
   Score: 5-1 Owls
   Goals: Travis (2), Simon, Nish, Andy
   Goaltender: Jeremy
   Turning Point: Dmitri sends Travis in alone and Travis snaps shot in off crossbar to give Owls 2-1 lead.

2. Owls versus Beauport Nordiques
   Score: 2-2 tie
   Goals: Sarah (2)
   Goaltender: Jeremy
   Turning Point: Sarah ties game with brilliant rush, pulls goalie and scores on backhand.
3. Owls versus Vermont Burlington Bears
   Score: 9-3 Owls
   Goals: Sarah (7 – ties Guy Lafleur's record), Fahd, Jesse
   Goaltender: Jenny
   Turning Point: Owls need to win by five goals to reach final, and Sarah plays game of her life, tying Lafleur's old record with an astonishing seven-goal performance.
4. Owls versus Beauport Nordiques (Championship Game)
   Score: 2-1 Owls
   Goals: Travis, Nish
   Goaltender: Jeremy
   Turning Point: Nish plays defensive game of his life, and scores winning goal on Dmitri's rebound.
   OWLS WIN CHAMPIONSHIP!

Hometown Play, Tamarack
1. Owls versus Orillia
   Score: 3-1 Orillia
   Goals: Sarah
   Goaltender: Jenny
   Turning Point: Orillia goaltender stands on head, stops Dmitri on two breakaways.
2. Larry Ulmar Fundraising Game
   Toronto Maple Leafs Legends (plus Muck Munro) versus The Flying Fathers
   Score: Unknown
   Goals: Muck scores final goal of game off crossbar.
3. Screech Owls versus Orillia
   Score: 5-1 Owls
   Goals: Dmitri, Sarah, Travis, Wilson, Nish
   Goaltender: Jeremy
   Turning Point: Nish decides to play, has sore leg frozen for game. Data makes appearance at game, inspiring team.

Junior Olympics Hockey Tournament, Nagano, Japan
1. Owls versus Sapporo Mighty Ducks
   Score: 5-4 Owls
   Goals: Sarah, Andy, Dmitri, Fahd, Liz
   Goaltender: Jenny, two periods; Nish, third period
   Turning Point: Nish makes fluke save to preserve victory.
2. Owls versus Matsumoto Sharks
   Score: 6-3 Owls
   Goals: Liz, Sarah, Dmitri, Travis, Wilson, Simon
   Goaltender: Jenny
   Turning Point: With score tied 3-3, Sarah takes charge, setting up linemates Travis and Dmitri and scoring once herself.
3. Owls versus Lake Placid Olympians (Championship Game)
   Score: 4-3 Owls
   Goals: Simon, Sarah, Andy, Travis
   Goaltender: Jenny; Nish replaces Jenny after she is injured
   Turning Point: Nish makes unbelievable barehanded save to preserve the win.
   OWLS WIN JUNIOR OLYMPICS GOLD MEDAL!

Drumheller Invitational Peewee Tournament
1. Owls versus Hanna Hurricanes
   Score: 6-3 Owls
   Goals: Travis, Andy, Fahd, Jesse, Wilson, Dmitri
   Goaltender: Jeremy
   Turning Point: Kelly Block "mixes the lines" and Owls almost blow their 5-0 lead until Sarah leads rush and sets up Dmitri for pretty goal.
2. Owls versus Winnipeg Werewolves
   Score: 5-3 Werewolves
   Goals: Sarah, Wilson, Jesse
   Goaltender: Jenny, Jeremy
   Turning Point: From opening face-off Owls cannot get used to Kelly Block's line changes, and lose to a far inferior team.
3. Owls versus Prince Albert Predators
   Score: 3-2 Owls
   Goals: Dmitri, Fahd, Nish
   Goaltender: Jenny
   Turning Point: Fahd ties the game on lucky play; tries to pass to Wilson, but puck fans off his stick into net.
4. Owls versus Lethbridge Blazers ("B" Championship Game)
   Score: 2-1 Owls (in overtime)
   Goals: Simon, Nish
   Goaltender: Jenny, Jeremy
   Turning Point: Muck comes to Drumheller to coach final game – Nish scores in overtime.
   OWLS WIN CHAMPIONSHIP!

Little Stanley Cup, Ottawa
1. Owls versus Rideau Rebels
   Score: 2-2 tie
   Goals: Dmitri, Fahd
   Goaltender: Jeremy
   Turning Point: Owls fail to protect their lead, allowing little James Groves of Rebels to sneak in and deke Jeremy for tying goal.
2. Owls versus Sudbury Minors
   Score: 7-0 Owls
   Goals: Dmitri, Andy, Sarah, Travis, Jesse, Liz, Simon
   Goaltender: Jenny
   Turning Point: Dmitri scores on first shift on clean breakaway.
3. Owls versus Vancouver Mountain
   Score: 4-3 Owls (in overtime)
   Goals: Sam, Fahd, Dmitri, Sarah
   Goaltender: Jenny Staples.
   Turning Point: Sam sends high long pass in O.T. to send Sarah in alone for winning goal.
4. Owls versus Rideau Rebels (Championship Game)
   Score: 2-1 Owls
   Goals: Andy, Sam
   Goaltender: Jeremy
   Turning Point: Travis uses Joe Hall's stick and famous "heel pass" to send puck back to pinching Sam, who steps around sliding goaltender and roofs shot.
   OWLS WIN CHAMPIONSHIP!

"3-on-3" International Peewee Competition, Vancouver
1. Lars, Dmitri, Sam play Seattle. Owls win 11-3.
2. Travis, Nish, Sarah play Portland Panthers. Owls win.
3. Travis, Nish, Sarah play Boston. Owls win 9-6.
4. Fahd, Gordie, Sam play Arrowhead Rangers. Owls win.

5. Travis's team versus Fahd's team, final.
   Score: Fahd's side 13, Travis' side 12 (shootout to decide)
   Goaltenders: Jeremy for Travis's team; Jenny for Fahd's.
   Turning Point: Sam scored in the shootout, Nish failed.

Big Apple International Peewee Tournament, New York City
1. Owls versus Long Island Selects
   Score: 6-0 Owls
   Goals: Dmitri (2), Travis (2), Nish (2)
   Goaltender: Jeremy
   Turning Point: Sam sets Dmitri up for first goal, Owls never look back.
2. Owls versus Detroit Wheels
   Score: 6-5 Owls
   Goals: Dmitri, Nish (2), Andy, Fahd, Derek
   Goaltender: Jenny
   Turning Point: Nish scores spectacular goal in dying seconds of game.
3. Owls versus Chicago Young Blackhawks
   Score: 5-4 Owls
   Goals: Travis, Mario, Sam, Jesse, Andy
   Goaltender: Jenny
   Turning Point: Sam scores winning goal on hard slapper in off crossbar and post.
4. Owls versus Detroit Wheels (Championship Game)
   Score: 5-4, Owls (in overtime)
   Goals: Mario, Sarah, Derek, Simon, Nish
   Goaltender: Jeremy
   Turning Point: In sudden-death overtime, Nish scores his treasured "Bure" goal.
   OWLS WIN CHAMPIONSHIP!

Screech Owls Peewee Lacrosse, Tamarack
1. Owls versus Toronto Mini-Rock
   Score: 19-8 Mini-Rock
   Goals: Sarah (3), Travis, four others.
   Goaltender: Nish
   Turning Point: Experienced Toronto team dominates from opening draw.
2. Owls versus Brantford Warriors
   Score: 7-7 tie
   Goals: Dmitri, Andy, Simon, Sam, Travis (2), Wilson
   Goaltender: Nish
   Turning Point: Travis ties game in final moments with "Muck Munro" move.
3. Owls versus Watertown Seaway
   Score: Owls 22, Seaway 5
   Scoring: Jesse Highboy leads way with four goals, four assists.
   Goaltender: Nish.
   Turning Point: Owls dominate from opening draw.
4. Owls versus Toronto Mini-Rock (Championship Game)
   Score: 14-13 Owls (in overtime)
   Scoring: Fahd, Dmitri (2), Sam, Travis, Nish, eight others.
   Goaltender: Nish
   Turning Point: Nish leaves crease and runs length of floor to score goal that wins the provincial championship.
   OWLS WIN CHAMPIONSHIP!

ROY MACGREGOR

Roy MacGregor is the author of several classics in the literature of hockey. *Home Game* (written with Ken Dryden) and *The Home Team* were both number-one national bestsellers. He has also written the game's best-known novel, *The Last Season*. Roy MacGregor is now a senior columnist for the *National Post*. He lives in Kanata, Ontario.

GREG BANNING

Greg Banning has been working as an illustrator for over ten years, specializing in book illustration and commercial work. Recent credits, apart from all the covers for the Screech Owls Series, include a *Maclean's* magazine cover and illustrations for Fox Sports, Microsoft, and Molson Breweries. He lives in Toronto, Ontario.

Be sure to visit the Screech Owls Web site at

www.screechowls.com